BURT FRANKLIN: RESEARCH & SOURCE WORKS SERIES 828
American Classics in History and Social Science 208

COLONIAL OPPOSITION TO IMPERIAL

AUTHORITY DURING THE FRENCH

AND INDIAN WAR

COLONIAL OPPOSITION TO IMPERIAL AUTHORITY DURING THE FRENCH AND INDIAN WAR

BY

EUGENE IRVING McCORMAC, Ph.D.

BURT FRANKLIN
NEW YORK

Published by LENOX HILL Pub. & Dist. Co. (Burt Franklin)
235 East 44th St., New York, N.Y. 10017
Originally Published: 1911
Reprinted: 1971
Printed in the U.S.A.

S.B.N.: 8337-23138
Library of Congress Card Catalog No. 73-172188
Burt Franklin: Research and Source Works Series 828
American Classics in History and Social Science 208

Reprinted from the original edition in the Wesleyan University
Library.

COLONIAL OPPOSITION TO IMPERIAL AUTHORITY DURING THE FRENCH AND INDIAN WAR

EUGENE IRVING McCORMAC

I. GENERAL VIEW

From the standpoint of constitutional history the period covered by the French and Indian War deserves a more careful and exhaustive study than has been given it by those who have written upon American colonial history. Only recently has a book appeared that seems to grasp the true relation of this period to the stormy one which followed it. Beer in his *British Colonial Policy, 1754-1765,* has given a valuable treatment of the policy of the mother country, and has incidentally touched upon the peculiar ideas and characteristics of the colonists; but the subject with which he deals necessarily does not include a study of constitutional development within the colonies.

Many writers have pointed out a connection between this war and the American Revolution by showing how the expulsion of the French and the incurring of a war debt furnished an excuse for the new colonial policy inaugurated by the Tory party in England. There are, however, many other questions which connect the two movements as vitally, if more remotely, as those usually discussed.

In a recent publication it is explicitly stated that "England and America entered on a dispute as to the distribution of power and the principles of government'"[1] with the passage of the Stamp Act. It is more nearly true to say that the Stamp Act and others which followed it were the result of disputes which arose in connection with every phase of the war with France. It is not contended that all of the anti-imperial and independent ideas of the colonists originated during this war, for many of them appeared earlier; but never before had the Americans so thoroughly elucidated their ideas on constitutional questions, and never before had they so clearly defined the position which they meant to maintain.

Hardly an issue which disturbed the relations between colonies and mother country between the passage of the Stamp Act and the Declaration of Independence was new. These issues had in one form or another been thrashed over in the controversies of the various assemblies with their governors, and the opinions of the colonists concerning them were formed and crystallized. The grounds upon which the colonists claimed exemption from British taxation and restrictions in the later period were by no means new; they had been asserted again and again in substantially the same terms during the war with France. The conditions in the two periods were similar and they called forth similar ideas, protests, and demands on the part of the Americans. In both cases the mother country attempted to procure assistance and to exact obedience from the colonies, and these attempts were resisted by the latter, who contended that such interference by England was an attack upon their long cherished "rights." That a declaration of independence and a separation did not come in the earlier period was due more to the want of a well-defined policy on either side o᷄ the Atlantic than to an absence of independent ideas in the colonies. This tendency to resist authority was more pronounced in some colonies than in others, and it took some time to develop a policy of concerted action; but it existed, nevertheless, in all of them, and it needed only additional pressure on the part of crown officials to develop this tendency into armed resistance.

---

[1] McLaughlin, *The Confederation and the Constitution*, 313-314.

The object of attack depended upon the character of the colonial government, in other words, upon the source of outside restraint. In proprietary colonies it was the alleged usurpations of the proprietor which must be opposed and defeated. If the proprietor could be overthrown entirely, so much the better. In these colonies there were usually unstinted professions of loyalty to the king, whose good will might be of service in overthrowing the proprietor. In royal colonies it was the governor who was continually accused of trampling under foot the "rights of his Majesty's faithful and loyal subjects." In the charter colonies there was little friction between the legislative and executive branches of government, for both were elected by and responsible to the people, but there was the same determination to preserve all charter rights and to acquire others if possible. Whatever the source, all outside authority must be resisted. When, at the close of the French and Indian War, Parliament became the instrument for enforcing such authority, the colonies at last united in common effort to resist and finally to overthrow all British control.

But coupled with this tenacious insistence upon acquired rights was another trait of the colonists which weakened materially their power of resistance. This was their utter lack of unity, their limited horizon, and their jealousy of one another.[2] The spirit of patriotism and national loyalty in the modern sense seems to have been almost entirely lacking. In a sense they gloried in being Englishmen and they hated the common enemy; but whenever the general welfare of the empire required them to sacrifice any of their cherished rights (however small) or to abandon a profitable trade with the enemy, they invariably chose the policy best suited to their own individual interests. This want of unity continued during the period which followed the war with France, but it was overcome in part on the eve of

---

[2] Burnaby, whose account of actual conditions is more valuable than his prophecies, wrote in 1759: ". . . . fire and water are not more heterogeneous than the different colonies in North America. Nothing can exceed the jealousy and emulation which they possess in regard to each other." *Travels*, in Pinkerton, *Voyages*, xiii, 751-752.

the Revolution by the efficient work of the committees of correspondence. These committees were effective instruments of agitation. They aroused public opinion and centered it upon the common danger. They caused local grievances, such as the closing of Boston harbor, to be adopted by other colonies. By spreading information and molding public opinion they created enthusiasm for the cause and overcame, for a time at least, the indifference which was so apparent during the French war.

When Governor Dinwiddie of Virginia learned from the defiant answer given to Major Washington in 1753 that the French meant to back their pretensions by force, he called upon the other colonies for assistance. "But the colonies, alas!" exclaimed a contemporary writer, "were sunk into a profound lethargy; and, resigned to stupidity and slumbering, appeared insensible of the threatening danger."[3] This charge, though severe, is substantiated by the records of the various colonies. They underrated the power of the French. They knew little and cared less about the western country, and they even questioned the title of the British crown to these lands.[4]

None knew better than the French the unprepared condition of the English colonists and their want of unity. The French considered early occupation and a defensive position of greater importance than the larger numbers of the English. "They declare without reserve," wrote Governor Dinwiddie, "that altho' we are vastly superior to them in Numbers, yet they can take and secure the Co't'y before we can agree to hinder them."[5] Still stronger evidence is found in a letter from Duquesne himself in which he said "The Governors of New England [mean-

---

[3] *Review of Military Operations,* in *Coll. Mass. Hist. Soc.,* ser. 1, viii, 72, 73.

[4] *Ibid.*

[5] Dinwiddie to Secretary Robinson, June 8, 1754. *Col. Rec. of N. C.,* v, 129. In writing to Governor DeLancey of New York for troops, Dinwiddie says that if the colonies concur "I shall hope the Consequences will be to show our Enemies how far they were mistaken in their Sarcasm they threw out, that tho' they owned, We could bring two men to their one, yet, that we were too slow, and disconnected, to hinder the progress of their Undertakings." Jan. 29, 1754. *Pa. Arch.,* ser. 2, vi, 179-180.

ing, probably, all the English colonies], besides being independent one of the other, cannot levy troops without an order of the King of Great Britain,[6] and you will have observed by Mr Washington's Journal that all the Provinces have furnished a quota to his detachment. I know, moreover, that the Quakers, who never make war, have also furnished their contingent.'"[7] The obvious meaning of this letter is that he considered such measures illegal, and mere bluster on the part of the colonists.

The French colonists and army were more directly under the control of the king, and, as they did not possess so many "rights" which must be defended, their military operations could be conducted with secrecy and dispatch. In the British colonies every plan had to be fought over in the assemblies before it could even be attempted, and the enemy always had ample opportunity to learn its details in advance.[8]

As Virginia took a greater interest in the Ohio country than the other colonies, she was naturally the first to act in its defense, and her governor, Dinwiddie, at once took steps to repel the invaders. But his enthusiasm was checked from the beginning by his reluctant assembly. They voted £1000 for raising and equipping three hundred men for defending the frontier, but the governor complained that they "were much divided" and failed to do as much as he had asked.[9] The surrounding colonies, however, were still less generous, for Dinwiddie had written only a week before to Secretary Robinson that "every Gov't except No. Caro. has amus'd me with Expectations that have proved fruitless, and at length refused to give any Supply, unless in such a manner as must render it ineffectual.'"[10]

The Pennsylvania assembly answered their governor's appeal for aid with a reply that was characteristic of their attitude throughout the war. They refused to vote assistance because

---

[6] War was not formally declared until May, 1756.

[7] *Pa. Arch.*, ser 2, vi, 173. Duquesne to DeMachault, Oct. 28, 1754.

[8] *Coll. Mass. Hist. Soc.*, ser. 1, vii, 161-162.

[9] *Col. Rec. of N. C.*, v, 110. To President Rowan of North Carolina, March 23, 1754.

[10] *Ibid.*, 129.

it had not been made clear to them that the subjects of a foreign prince had erected forts "within the undoubted Limits of this Government." The limits "had not been ascertained to y^eir satisfaction."[11] As the war progressed it seemed difficult to prove this or anything else to their satisfaction.[12]

The assembly of New York required equally strong proof of ownership before they would vote aid to the king. "It appears," they said in an address to the lieutenant-governor, "by papers your Honor has been pleased to communicate to us, that the French have built a fort at a place called French Creek, at a considerable distance from the river Ohio, which may, but does not by any evidence or information appear to us to be an invasion of any of his Majesty's colonies."[13] This was rather an impertinent stand to take when the British government had already decided that its territory had been invaded. The assembly finally decided to vote £1000 for the purpose of sending two companies to Virginia, but the money was to be raised in a manner which the council declared contrary to the king's instructions and therefore refused to allow. The perennial quarrel over a permanent salary for the governor was also in progress, and when the present bill was not allowed by the council, the assembly refused to pass another. DeLancey thought that the council was also at fault in not waiving its grounds during this critical situation, but the king severely criticised the assembly for their declaration and their refusal on such "trifling" grounds to grant aid.[14]

---

[11] *Pa. Arch., 1748-56*, ii, 235. Resolution of the assembly, March 8, 1754.

[12] Another excuse given for refusing aid was that the Earl of Holdernesse had asked for aid against the French *within* their respective provinces, and as the boundary line between Pennsylvania and Virginia had never been settled, they feared that they might invade Virginia in pursuit of the enemy. They would wait, therefore, to see what Virginia would do. The governor explained that the earl had meant to ask for aid to defend all of the king's lands, and that the governor of Virginia had asked for assistance, but the assembly refused to be convinced and adjourned without granting the aid. *Pa. Col. Rec.*, v, 763-765.

[13] *Coll. Mass. Hist. Soc.*, ser. 1, vii, 72-73. Address of the New York Assembly, April 23, 1754.

[14] *Pa. Arch.*, ser. 2, vi, 188, 192, 196. Letters of DeLancey and Secretary Robinson.

During the entire summer of 1754 Governor Dinwiddie was unable to procure sufficient assistance to enable him to assume the offensive. Governor Sharpe, on November 5, wrote to Lord Bury that Dinwiddie, having secured but three hundred men from Virginia, two companies from New York, one from South Carolina, and three hundred men from North Carolina, was forced to abandon his plans for the present.[15] It will be shown later that even this nominal assistance was of little value.

When we consider that the ravages of the French and Indians were at least as disastrous to the colonies as to the empire in general, and that it was their property and lives that were at stake, it does not seem that the requirements of the mother country were unreasonable. England asked that the troops be supplied with provisions by the colonies and that the officers be conveyed from place to place. The colonial governments were required to assist in executing the orders of British officers for quartering troops, impressing carriages, and equipping forts. In addition, each colony was asked to contribute to a common fund for the general protection.[16] Of course both sides considered that England owed the colonies protection from foreign enemies in return for obedience and advantages she received from the colonies[17]; nevertheless no theory of this kind could excuse the conduct of colonial assemblies in allowing the inhabitants to be butchered while they were haggling over mere technicalities. The governors in many cases were equally culpable in obstructing legislation for trivial reasons. Some of the governors adhered too rigidly to the letter of their instructions, or even enlarged upon them, which tended to intensify the discord.

The British government looked to the governors to enforce its orders, and the position of those officials was by no means an enviable one. In general the governors tried to perform their duties to the crown, but as Dinwiddie wrote in 1754, "A Governor in the Discharge of His Duty to his King and Country, is

---

[15] *Corresp. of Gov. Sharpe,* i, 115.

[16] *Ibid.,* 108, Secretary Robinson to Sharpe.

[17] See Beer, *British Colonial Policy, 1754-1765,* chap. 1.

much to be pittied, when its considered his Transactions with an obstinate Assembly; Full of their own opinions, & entirely deaf to Argument & Reason.''[18] This of course is only a governor's side of the controversy, but the records bear out his statement.

From the beginning the New England colonies, particularly Massachusetts, showed public spirit and liberality in furnishing aid to repel the enemy,[19] and some of the southern governors in desperation asked them for aid when the southern assemblies would do nothing for their own defense. Governor Sharpe of Maryland admitted that he had little reason for expecting assistance from New England ''while they see us in a State of almost total inactivity or Supineness,'' but seeing no other means of getting supplies he asked aid from New Hampshire, Rhode Island, and Connecticut.[20] He had little faith in the loyalty of any of the colonial legislatures, for in the same letter he added ''I have learnt not to entertain very sanguine hopes of the Resolutions of American Assemblies . . . As often as they have been convened urged and intreated to aid each other in defending his Majesty's Territories & their own Properties so often almost have they as it were unanimously refused to provide against the Dangers that threaten them or endeavored to cast the Odium on their respective Gover[rs] by laying them under a necessity of rejecting such Bills as were presented them with the specious Titles of Acts for His Majesty's Service & the better Defense & Security of the British Colonies.'' This letter was not written for publication nor for the purpose of exerting influence in official circles. It was a private letter to his brothers and no doubt expressed the governor's sincere opinion of the situation. In it he seems to have struck the key-note of the policy of many of the colonial governments, particularly of Maryland and Pennsylvania. This policy was to make effusive professions of generosity to the king, and then to claim that it

---

[18] *Corresp. of Gov. Sharpe,* i, 97. Dinwiddie to Sharpe, Sept. 5, 1754.

[19] *Ibid.,* 110, Sharpe to W. and J. Sharpe.

[20] *Ibid.*

was due wholly to arbitrary instructions from proprietors or vetoes by governors that they were unable to assist. In the two provinces just mentioned the assemblies saw in the disastrous conditions of the time an opportunity to weaken if not entirely to overthrow proprietary rule.

When the aggressive plans of the French became known, those in authority, both in England and America, began to consider some form of concerted action to be taken either by the colonies acting alone or by the colonies acting under parliamentary regulations. The governors, generally, believed that little could be accomplished unless Parliament should assume control and enforce its authority. Such a plan had been suggested to Newcastle by Bedford in 1748 as a result of the independent attitude of the colonies during King George's War. He recommended that a strong man be put at the head of the Board of Trade and the Earl of Halifax was chosen for the position.[21] Without a vigorous Board new laws would not bring about the desired results.

When Halifax assumed office he found letters from various colonial governors complaining of insubordination and republican tendencies in the colonies. The governor of New York could not "meet the Assembly, without danger of exposing the king's authority" and himself to contempt.[22] Governor Glen of South Carolina reported that "Here, levelling principles prevail; the frame of civil government is unhinged; a governor, if he would be idolized, must betray his trust; . . . . to preserve the dependence of America in general, the Constitution must be new modelled."[23] Similar complaints came from Massachusetts, Virginia, Pennsylvania, and New Jersey.[24] Though somewhat exaggerated, these many charges could hardly fail to have weight with the home government.

Halifax proceeded with more energy than tact to instruct

[21] Bancroft, *History of the United States*, ed. 22, iv, 36.
[22] Clinton to Bedford, Oct. 20, 1748. Quoted by Bancroft, iv, 36.
[23] Letters of Glen to Bedford, July 27 and Oct. 10, 1748. Quoted by Bancroft, iv, 38.
[24] Bancroft, iv, 38-40.

the governors to enforce a more rigid policy, but as the encroachments of the French soon occupied their attention, little was attained except to arouse suspicion in the colonies and to make them more determined to oppose any centralizing measures of the British government.

When hostilities began in 1754, General Shirley, who from the first was one of the most active governors, doubted that the colonies would ever agree on quotas and other matters of assistance unless the proportions were fixed in England. Past experience, he said, taught that they had never been able to agree on these matters, and unless they were now fixed by the king and enforced by law, no adequate protection could be expected. Quotas had been fixed in the reign of William III, but conditions had changed since then. In his opinion no union of the colonies except one controlled by England would ever accomplish the desired results.[25] Shirley was one of the first to suggest a union of the colonies and he urged that delegates to the Albany convention be given adequate powers.[26]

The Albany convention and the reception of the plan there adopted demonstrated that no union could be formed by the colonies that would be satisfactory to themselves or to the British government. All agreed that a union of some kind was desirable, but neither the colonies nor England was willing to concede the things necessary to bring it about. The colonies agreed on the necessity of winning the good will of the Indians at this time, and nearly all of them voted money with little hesitation to secure it, but Massachusetts alone gave her delegates full power to enter into a union.[27] New Jersey refused either to

---

25 *Pa. Arch.*, ser. 2, iv, 174-177. Shirley to Holdernesse, Jan. 7, 1754. Governor Hamilton of Pennsylvania had declared as early as 1753 that there would be no union unless the ministry should compel the colonies to form one. All former attempts had failed because of the "mutual and injudicious jealousies" of the colonies. He added that the principles "either real or pretended" of the Pennsylvania assembly will prevent its entering into a union or doing anything of a warlike nature. *Pa. Col. Rec.*, vi, 632.

26 *Pa. Col. Rec.*, iv, 19. Shirley to Hamilton, March 4, 1754.

27 *Pa. Arch., 1748-56*, ii, 137. Commission given by Governor Shirley; *Pa. Arch.*, ser. 2, vi, 213-218, Shirley to Robinson.

vote money or to send delegates to Albany, giving as excuse
that she had no commercial relations with the Six Nations. This
excuse was pronounced frivolous by the Board of Trade who
censured the colony for its indifference and lack of obedience
to the king's orders.[28] Pennsylvania gave full power to her
commissioners to conclude a treaty with the Indians and to
give money,[29] but nothing was said about a union with the other
colonies.[30] Rhode Island gave her delegates authority to *consult*
on methods of securing the good will of the Indians and protection against the French "And in General, as far as the abil-
ities of this Government will permit, to act in Conjunction with
the said Commissioners in every thing Necessary for the good
of his Majesty's Subjects in these Parts."[31] This qualified
authority was little better than none at all, and the commission
of the Connecticut delegates was equally devoid of authority.
They were to meet and consult with the other commissioners and
"to use and pursue proper measures in pursuance of their
(your) instructions from the said General Assembly."[32] Even
the appointment of delegates was made by the assembly and
not by the governor. The New Hampshire commissioners were
given full power to conclude a treaty with the Indians, but
none to enter into a union.[33] Maryland voted £500 for the
Indians, but on any scheme of defense her delegates were given
no authority to act. They were simply to "observe the propositions" and report all plans to Governor Sharpe, but to agree
to no plan for men or forts.[34] Virginia sent no delegates to
Albany because Governor Dinwiddie was himself negotiating
with the Indians, but about a year afterward, when General

---

[28] *N. J. Arch.*, ser. 1, viii, part 1, 294-295.

[29] The assembly was willing to vote "a small Present" but could not
be expected to "make it very large at this Time" on account of heavy
expenses. Answer to the governor. *Pa. Col. Rec.*, v, 749.

[30] Commission. *Pa. Arch., 1748-56*, ii, 142-143.

[31] *Ibid.*, 141-142.

[32] *Ibid.*, 140-141.

[33] *Ibid.*, 138.

[34] *Ibid.*, 139-140.

Shirley asked the assembly to send commissioners to meet those from other colonies, they "immediately made Resolve against it."[35]

It is well known that none of the colonies accepted the plan of union prepared by the convention at Albany because they considered that by it too much power would be taken from their hands. Some of them voted it down with silent contempt, while a few strenuously opposed it as a serious menace to their liberties. A committee of the Connecticut assembly appointed to consider the plan thought that the general taxing power given to the President-General and Council was "a very extraordinary thing, and against the rights and privileges of Englishmen in general." It would be an "innovation" and "breach on charter privileges" and "greatly discourage and dishearten his Majesty's good subjects." If the President-General were given power to appoint military officers, they said, the "youth would not enlist."[36] The assembly stated that the Connecticut commissioners opposed the plan while at Albany and refused assent to it,[37] but both Franklin and Hutchinson who were members of the convention said that it was unanimously adopted.[38]

Although Massachusetts gave her delegates larger powers than other colonies, the plan of union when submitted for ratification was rejected. A "large body of people assembled in town-meeting" at Boston to consider the plan disapproved by a decided majority. Dr. William Clarke, one of the number, wrote Franklin that the projected plan for union was a "scheme for the destroying the liberties and privileges of every British subject upon the continent."[39]

The Pennsylvania assembly denied the binding force of any general union even in Indian affairs, asserting that "we con-

---

[35] *Pa. Arch., 1748-56,* ii, 446.

[36] *Coll. Mass. Hist. Soc.,* ser. 1, vii, 208-209.

[37] *Ibid.,* 213.

[38] Franklin, *Works,* i, 177; Hutchinson, *History of Massachusetts Bay,* iii, 23. Another contemporary said that "every member of the congress, except Mr. DeLancey," approved the plan. *Coll. Mass. Hist. Soc.,* ser. 1, vii, 77.

[39] *Coll. Mass. Hist. Soc.,* ser. 1, vi, 85-86.

sider that no Propositions for an Union of the Colonies in Indian
Affairs can effectually answer the good Purposes, or be binding
farther than they are confirmed by Laws enacted under the
several Governments comprized in that Union.''[40]

Rhode Island like Connecticut saw in the Albany plan a
menace to her charter rights and took vigorous steps to defeat
it. Her agent in England was ''directed to be upon his watch,
and if any thing shall be moved in Parliament, respecting the
plan for a union of his Majesty's northern[41] colonies, projected
at Albany, which may have a tendency to infringe on our char-
tered privileges, that he use his utmost endeavors to get it put
off, until such time as the government is furnished with a copy,
and have opportunity of making answer thereto.''[42]   Parliament, however, took no action in the matter.

The part of the Albany plan which the colonies considered
most dangerous was that which gave taxing power to the Grand
Council and President-General. They ignored the fact that this
council was to possess the initiative and that its members were
to be chosen from the colonies by the representatives of the
people. This taxing power was to be limited to the levying of
''duties, imposts or taxes'' for general purposes only. It would
make the general government self-supporting within its own
limited sphere, but in other respects the integrity and autonomy
of the separate governments would have remained as before.
After years of bitter experience it was found necessary to grant
such powers to the new federal government. It would be idle
to speculate on the probable effect that the adoption of the
Albany plan would have had in obviating or postponing the
Revolution, for there was never any probability that such a
measure would be acceptable to either side.

The British government and British officials in America opposed the plan prepared at Albany because it did not give

---

[40] *Pa. Col. Rec.,* vi, 45.

[41] Besides the plan embracing all of the colonies, another plan was
proposed at Albany for a union of six of the northern colonies.   *Coll.
Mass. Hist. Soc.,* ser. 1, vii, 203.

[42] Arnold, *History of Rhode Island,* ii, 191.

sufficient control to the mother country. General Shirley severely criticized it and declared that powers were assumed that belonged to the king. He likened it to the governments of Connecticut and Rhode Island which were practically independent of the crown. The latter especially had, in his opinion, abused its freedom. He believed that any attempt at union by the colonies themselves must prove futile because of their "different conditions, situations, circumstances and tempers." He did not believe that the commissioners who drafted the Albany plan had any expectation that it would be adopted; and if it had been adopted, it could never have been executed.[43]   Governor Morris of Pennsylvania pronounced the plan too republican in principle, giving the crown little or no authority, and he did not wonder that it "was not relished at home." He rightly observed that any effective union must permit the general government to employ the colonial forces when and where it might be necessary.[44]   This was a point which the colonists were never willing to concede, and their obstinacy hindered military operations throughout the war.

A treaty with the Six Nations was the immediate object of the meeting at Albany, and, as above stated, several of the colonies voted money and gave authority to their delegates on this subject while they refused to commit themselves on the question of union. The British government, also, fully realized the importance of an Indian alliance. In a report to the king on the Albany convention, the Board of Trade pointed out how impossible it was for individual colonies to deal successfully with the Indians, however good the intentions of any colony might be. New York had, up to this time, been the colony chiefly concerned with Indian affairs, but for various reasons—including duplicity and selfish dealing of the New York commissioners

---

[43] *Pa. Arch.*, ser. 2, vi, 213-218; *N. Y. Col. Hist. Docs.*, vi, 930. Shirley to Secretary Robinson, Dec. 24, 1754. Hutchinson says in his *History of Massachusetts Bay* (iii, 23) that "some of the delegates who agreed to it in Albany doubted whether it would ever be approved of by the king, the parliament, or any of the American assemblies."

[44] *Pa. Arch., 1748-56*, ii, 499. Morris to Shirley.

—the Indians had lost faith in the English. The French had grasped the opportunity and by pursuing the opposite policy were winning the friendship of the Indians. For these reasons the Board of Trade asked the king to take charge of Indian affairs as the only remedy that could forestall the French.[45] Members of this board had already urged the importance of the friendship of the Six Nations and criticised the colonies for not exerting themselves to secure it. In a letter to DeLancey of New York they said, "The preserving and securing the friendship of these Indians is in the present situation of affairs an object of the greatest Importance it is from the steady adherence of these Indians to the British Interests that not only New York but all the other Northern Colonys have hitherto been secured from the fatal effects of the encroachments of a foreign power, and without their friendship and assistance all our efforts to check and disappoint the present view of this power may prove ineffectual." The advantages of such a treaty, they said, "are so apparent that we are at a loss to guess at the motives for the conduct of those Colony's who have declined joining in the treaty with them."[46] As nearly every colony had expressed an opinion that a general union was absolutely necessary, and as a convention such as the one held at Albany was the only method of forming one, the Board of Trade was both surprised and disappointed with the indifference and obstinacy of the colonies.[47]

Inability of the colonies to form a union for common defense made a bad impression upon the Indians whose friendship they were seeking. The Indians doubted the sincerity of the English and their ability to act with vigor and unanimity against the French. They were, therefore, not eager to form an alliance with the English.[48] No one could blame the Indians for not

[45] Report, Oct. 29, 1754, *N. Y. Col. Hist. Docs.*, vi, 917-918; *Pa. Arch.*, ser. 2, vi, 206-210. This recommendation was soon acted upon and Sir William Johnson was appointed colonel of the Six Nations.

[46] *N. Y. Col. Hist. Docs.*, vi, 845-846; *Pa. Arch.*, ser. 2, vi, 193.

[47] *Ibid.*

[48] Sir William Johnson, *Suggestions*, etc., *in Pa. Arch.*, ser. 2, vi, 204.

wishing to aid what must inevitably be the losing side, for defeat would leave them at the mercy of their long-standing enemy.

With such want of unity admitted on all sides, and with such indifference and jealousy of everything outside of their own immediate localities, it is not at all surprising that the call for men and money to carry on the war met with opposition in the various colonies. In general they seemed to look upon the war as a struggle for empire on the part of the two mother countries. If successful, England would reap the benefits and should therefore pay the expenses. The colonies most exposed might see some immediate advantage in the success of England, but even they as a rule preferred to let the enemy do his worst, and unhindered, rather than yield the smallest of their much cherished "rights." Not only did they guard against yielding anything to the British government, but even the most energetic of them watched carefully the actions of other colonies, each government jealous lest it might do more than its share. For this reason Governor Shirley urged the Earl of Holdernesse to have the quotas fixed in England. Massachusetts had done something, he said, but hesitated to do more until Connecticut and other colonies should evince a disposition to do their share.[49] Maryland waited to see what Virginia and Pennsylvania would do before she would vote supplies, and Governor Sharpe dryly remarked that Fort Du Quesne "I believe is too strong for me to reduce by Virtue of His Excellency's Commission without either Men, Artillery, Money or Provisions."[50]

Governor Morris of Pennsylvania ventured the opinion in 1755 that Braddock's army need not have been sent to America if the colonies had not been divided and jealous, and their assemblies made up of men "unacquainted with the nature of government, & hav(ing) private and selfish ends to answer."[51] Morris had written a short time before this to Braddock that "The Conduct of the Assemblies upon the Continent almost

---

[49] *Pa. Arch.*, ser. 2, vi, 174-177.

[50] *Corresp. of Gov. Sharpe*, i, 403. Sharpe to W. Sharpe, May 2, 1756.

[51] *Pa. Arch., 1748-56*, ii, 280.

without Exception has been so very absurd that they have suffered the French to take quiet Possession of the most advantageous Places, not only to answer the Purposes of a very extensive Indian Trade, but to enable them to protect their own Settlements and annoy ours; such are their Forts at Niagara, Crown Point, and the several ones upon Lake Erie, the River Ohio, and its Branches." The Indians, he added, had asked for aid, but the colonies would do nothing.[52]

Such were the conditions in the colonies when England called upon them for assistance in the war with the French. Public spirit and liberality could hardly be expected. It was not the expense alone which the colonies opposed (although according to a contemporary they were "parsimonious even to prodigality"),[53] but the whole system of imperial control. Each colony guarded jealously the "rights" which it prized more than the general welfare, and some of the assemblies saw in the urgent needs of the home government an opportunity to enlarge upon those "rights."

When hostilities with the French became inevitable, the king sent orders (October 7, 1754) to Governor Shirley of Massachusetts to enlist volunteers. All magistrates were required to assist in their official capacities.[54]

In the early part of the war royal orders required that only troops of proper age and size should be enlisted,[55] but before the struggle had proceeded far, almost any kind of troops was willingly accepted.

II. NEW ENGLAND
MASSACHUSETTS

In general the New England governments responded with more willingness and promptness than the other colonies. From

---

[52] *Pa. Col. Rec.*, vi, 336. See also *Review of Military Operations*, etc., *in Coll. Mass. Hist. Soc.*, ser. 1, vii, 75.

[53] *Coll. Mass. Hist. Soc.*, ser. 1, vii, 161-162.

[54] *Pa. Arch.*, ser. 2, ii, 686.

[55] Distrust of Catholics led the king to issue orders forbidding their enlistment. e.g. *Pa. Arch.*, ser. 2, ii, 691-693, 700-701.

the first they took the lead in active military operations.[56] Both
Massachusetts and Connecticut voted money liberally.[57] Massachusetts, especially, under the leadership of Governor Shirley,
took a prominent part in all of the northern campaigns. Shirley
was more popular than royal governors[58] in other colonies and
during his administration the assembly usually granted muni-
tions of war with little opposition. Shirley's success with his
assembly was due in part to his diplomatic policy in dealing
with them. "He generally urged the measures which he proposed to the assembly," said Hutchinson,[59] "as far as he could
without worrying them and putting them out of temper, and
no further." By representing to them that the money would
be repaid by England he induced many of the members to withdraw their opposition and vote for military grants.[60] In 1756.
when the assembly hesitated, Shirley again induced them to vote
aid by urging that the surest way to "obtain a compensation
for what they had already done would be by a further vigorous
exertion." When they pleaded want of ability to borrow money
on their credit to meet the present expense, Shirley met this
objection by loaning them £30,000 sterling which had been sent
over for the use of the royal troops.[61] Mr. Bollan, their agent
in London, made the most of this alleged poverty in urging
Parliament to reimburse the colony,[62] and contended that the
colony had exhausted its resources in financing the Crown Point
expedition. The fact that several of the members of the assembly

---

[56] *Coll. Mass. Hist. Soc.*, ser. 1, vi, 40; vii, 139; *Pa. Arch., 1748-56*, ii,
579; same, ser. 2, vi, 223-224; *Pa. Col. Rec.*, vi, 486.

[57] *Pa. Arch., 1748-56*, ii, 398. Delancey to Morris, Sept. 1, 1755.

[58] "With respect to the wisdom and equity of his administration, he
[Shirley] can boast the universal suffrage of a wise, free, jealous, and
moral people." *Coll. Mass. Hist. Soc.*, ser. 1, vii, 69.

[59] *History of Massachusetts Bay*, ii, 16.

[60] *Ibid.*, 29.

[61] *Ibid.*, 44, 45. He adds: "The province was never in better credit
than at this time. They could have borrowed enough to pay the charges
of the past and present year; but this mode of proceeding induced many
members to come into the measure. They were made to believe it tended
to facilitate the obtaining of a grant from parliament."

[62] *Coll. Mass. Hist. Soc.*, ser. 1, vi, 47.

were veterans of the Louisburg expedition made the governor's task much easier.[63]   The appointment of their governor as commander-in-chief which gave the colony a commanding position no doubt contributed to the public spirit of the assembly. An incident occurred in 1755 after the Crown Point expedition which illustrates their jealousy and desire for prestige. Shirley had induced the assembly to acquiesce in his appointment of Colonel Johnson of New York as commanding-general of the expedition by representing that he was the only man that could induce the Indians to join the English. Johnson was successful in an engagement with the French and captured a number of the enemy, including the French general. The Massachusetts assembly was greatly displeased because Johnson reported his success to New York instead of their own government. The assembly ordered the lieutenant-governor to ''acquaint general Johnson, that, as the Massachusetts province bore the greatest part of the charge and burden of the expedition, it ought to be considered as principal in all respects; and that all papers and advices of importance ought to be first sent to that province; and that the French general, and other prisoners of note, ought to be sent to Boston.''[64]

Besides voting men and money freely, the assembly at different times offered liberal bounties to volunteers and enacted adequate draft laws. No troops could be taken from the province without their own consent unless the removal was sanctioned by the assembly, but such authority was readily given in most cases. After Braddock's defeat they met in extra-legal session[65] and made provision for an additional force of two thousand men. They were not so punctilious in small matters as some of the other assemblies, and on several occasions tacitly allowed the governor and council to perform acts which, constitutionally, the assembly alone had power to do.[66]

---

[63] Hutchinson, *History of Massachusetts Bay*, iii, 28.

[64] *Ibid.*, 36

[65] See *ibid.* 34, for particulars.

[66] *Ibid.*, 58.

There were of course occasional murmurings concerning the heavy financial burden,[67] and serious trouble with Loudoun over the interpretation of the British quartering act seemed imminent in 1757, but controversies were, as a rule, amicably settled and did not prevent the assembly from doing all that could be reasonably expected of it. On one occasion only was there a threatened deadlock over the control and disbursement of money voted for military purposes. The assembly adopted a practice which prevailed in several of the other colonies of appropiating money to be paid to particular troops for a particular service and forbidding that it be used for any other purpose. Shirley had signed such bills, but Pownall who became governor in 1757 refused his assent to a bill of this kind, declaring it unconstitutional. He held out for several days, but the assembly would not yield the point and he at last signed it under protest.[68]

This episode passed unnoticed in England, and as the assembly had won their point, the military situation was not affected by it. In the early part of 1758 when a call came from Pitt for troops to invade Canada, the assembly responded by a unanimous vote to send seven thousand men to serve with the British regulars. They had high hopes of the success of the expedition and as Pownall wrote, "It was thought proper that this Province should set the example."[69] Pitt's promise of reimbursement no doubt had its influence on the members. Although England did not fully repay Massachusetts for the expense she had incurred during the war, the specie expended in the province and the increase in commerce compensated her, in part at least, for her liberal grants.[70]

CONNECTICUT

In Connecticut, as a result of popular government, liberal

---

[67] After the Crown Point expedition they at first declined to vote new supplies, declaring that "securing his majesty's territories is a design which his majesty only is equal to project and execute, *and the nation to support;* and that it cannot reasonably be expected that these infant plantations should engage as principals in the affair." Hutchinson, iii, 38.

[68] Hutchinson, iii, 66-67.

[69] *R. I. Col. Rec.,* vi, 136.

[70] Hutchinson, iii, 79.

powers were given by the assembly to executive officers. For
the same reason the assembly coöperated with the governor by
voting liberal grants of money and supplies. In 1755, when
General Shirley called on Connecticut to furnish a quota of
one thousand men for the Crown Point expedition, the assembly
voted to comply with the request, although they considered the
number relatively larger than the quotas of Massachusetts and
New York.[71] They even permitted New York to enlist three
hundred men in Connecticut for this expediton.[72] I have found
no similar instance in the records of any other colony. The
estimated expense to Connecticut of this expedition was reported
to the Board of Trade as over £6000 sterling.[73] When the Earl
of Loudoun called for troops in 1756 the Connecticut assembly
promptly voted the necessary men.[74] A few months later (January, 1757), however, they appointed a committee to confer with
the earl at Boston. This committee was given authority to
furnish men not to exceed one thousand two hundred and fifty,
but the number furnished must be governed by the quotas voted
by other New England colonies.[75] While the assembly's fear
of doing more than its share is evident in the succeeding years
of the war, nevertheless it showed public spirit and loyalty to
the cause.[76] The fact that even the most loyal colonies felt it
necessary to make such contingent grants only emphasized the
necessity of some central authority. Acts were passed for
quartering British troops and for protecting them from exor-
bitant prices.[77] In 1755, 1756, and again in 1758, the assembly

---

[71] *Col. Rec. of Conn.*, x, 336.

[72] *Ibid.*, 390.

[73] *Ibid.*, 624.

[74] *Ibid.*, 545, 555.

[75] *Ibid.*, 594-595.

[76] *Ibid.*, 598-599; xi, 93, and many scattered items in vols. x and xi,
for example, the following from vol. xi:

March, 1758, £30,000, p. 100.   March, 1760, £70,000, p. 351.
February, 1759, £20,000, p. 214.   March, 1761, £45,000, p. 482.
March, 1759, £40,000, p. 235.   March, 1762, £65,000, p. 615.
May, 1759, £10,000, p. 255.

[77] *Ibid.*, xi, 176, 190, 216, 304.

authorized the impressment of troops to complete the quotas.[78]
In October, 1755, the assembly appointed a "Committee of War"
and gave it full power to send out any number of troops it
thought necessary to defend the frontier towns and neighboring
provinces, and to do anything else necessary for defense.[79]   In
striking contrast to assemblies farther south, they gave the governor ample power in matters of appointments and the disbursement of money.[80]   There was consequently little friction
in internal affairs.

RHODE ISLAND

Rhode Island, like her sister charter colony, Connecticut,
voted men and money quite freely, and for the same reason
there was no clash between executive and legislative authority.
But here also is found the same determination to do relatively
no more than her neighbors.   On January 1, 1755, in response
to a letter from Sir Thomas Robinson, the assembly promptly
voted one hundred men and offered a bounty of £18 for enlistment.[81]   They voted a few days later to establish a lottery for
the purpose of raising £10,000 toward building Fort George.[82]
When, in March, General Shirley requested aid for the Crown
Point expedition the assembly immediately voted four hundred
men and £60,000 for expenses, but the act was to be effective
only on condition that other colonies did their share.   A "Committee of War" was appointed to purchase supplies and to look
after matters of defense.[83]   Despite the opposition of some
members who asserted that Rhode Island had done relatively
more than other colonies, additional grants of men and money
were made for this expedition.   Commissioners were chosen to
meet those from other colonies, and instead of dictating everything as was customary in royal and proprietary provinces, the

---

[78] *Col. Rec. of Conn.*, x, 398, 495; xi, 121.

[79] *Ibid.*, x, 319.

[80] *Ibid.*, 483.

[81] *R. I. Col. Rec.*, v, 404.

[82] *Ibid.*, 505.

[83] *Ibid.*, 418-426.

assembly gave the commissioners full power to assist other colonies during the present and future campaigns.[84] Their zeal brought them hearty commendation from the king.[85] Governor Hopkins informed Partridge, their agent in London, that the Crown Point campaign alone cost Rhode Island £15,000 sterling.[86]

Liberal grants were made in succeeding years. Laws were passed to promote enlistment by giving bounties, to enforce discipline by court-martial, and to prevent desertion.[87] Usually the assembly did not oppose the taking of troops to serve outside of the colony. In one instance they adopted a restrictive measure which called forth a well-merited rebuke from Loudoun, who asserted with good reason that the service of colonial troops on such terms would be more detrimental than beneficial.[88] The rebuke had the desired effect, for a few months later (August, 1757) the assembly voted to send one-sixth of their militia on the Lake George expedition, and the treasurer was authorized to "hire" money for their support.[89] The number of troops who served in the field in most cases fell short of the number voted. Dereliction of officers in charge of the draft, who accepted bribes in lieu of service, nullified the laws in many instances,[90] in spite of the good intentions of the assembly.

On the whole there seems to be little foundation for the charge often made against the two charter colonies by royal officials—that they were less loyal to the interests of the mother

---

[84] *R. I. Col. Rec.*, v, 433, 438, 448-449, 464.

[85] *Ibid.*, 467.

[86] *Ibid.*, 500. Memorial of Partridge to Board of Trade, April 2, 1756.

[87] *Ibid.*, 492; vi, 22, 34, 78, 129, and many later items.

[88] "The confining your men to any particular service, appears to me to be a preposterous measure. Our affairs are not in a situation to make it reasonable for any colony to be influenced by its particular interest . . . ." He agrees to treat the soldiers well, "But to engage that I will employ them in this or that particular place only, it is what I cannot do upon any terms; for I think it would be sure to be more prejudicial to the public than the whole benefit which we may expect from the provincial forces would countervail." Loudoun to Governor Hopkins, Jan. 29, 1757. *R. I. Col. Rec.*, vi, 17.

[89] *R. I. Col. Rec.*, vi, 75, 78.

[90] *Ibid.*, 137. Gen. Abercromby to Lieut. Gov. Gardner, March 15, 1758.

country than those colonies which enjoyed less freedom and autonomy. Compared with others, their attitude was loyal and generous.

New Hampshire

Of all New England colonies New Hampshire was most reluctant in voting assistance during the war. While the other New England assemblies responded more or less cheerfully[91] to calls from the commanding general, the assembly of New Hampshire always deliberated long and carefully before acting. Very often the assistance they did vote was too long delayed to be of much service. The disposition of the assembly to haggle over small points is very noticeable, but disputes with the governor never reached the intensity of similar contentions in the middle colonies. The harmony, however, was more apparent than real. When they denied a request of the governor they usually based their refusal on pleas of poverty or on a different interpretation of royal instructions. They did not deny British authority outright. The governor on his part did not resort to abusive language, but confined his arguments to the letter of his instructions, and usually in the end yielded to prevent the entire failure of desired measures. For these reasons an open breach was avoided.

As early as January, 1754, Governor Wentworth called the assembly to account for not including a suspending clause in their laws which would render them inoperative until approved by the king. In this province, he said, no law could become effective until it had been so approved.[92] The assembly ignored the protest, and necessity forced the governor to allow the practice to continue.

The suspending clause was considered a most arbitrary and unreasonable thing by all colonies in which it was required, and it was later included in the Declaration of Independence as one of the charges against the king. Like all veto power it was capable of being abused and no doubt was abused in some

[91] *N. H. Prov. Pap.*, vi, 499. Shirley to Wentworth, March 16, 1756.
[92] *Ibid.*, 232.

cases, but England considered it necessary to have some check on legislation, especially on laws for the extravagant issue of paper money.

When first asked to assist in the common defense the New Hampshire assembly expressed deep concern and loyalty, but pleaded poverty.[93] A little later they voted a small number of troops to serve for a few months in defending their own province. This short term of service and the uncertainty of additional grants made it impossible for the governor to form any definite plans.[94]

Much time was lost in waiting to see what other colonies—especially Massachusetts—were going to contribute. This made the small contributions of the legislative body tardy and less effective. They voted six hundred men in March of 1775, which they claimed was a much greater number than their just quota. They did it on account of critical times and this number was not to be a "Precedent" for future quotas. These troops were for the first Crown Point expedition and were to be "subsisted at the charge of this Province with provisions till they shall arrive at the place of Gen¹ Rendezvous and no longer."[95] The route over which the troops were marched did not suit the assembly so they declined to furnish additional men.[96] Some money, however, was voted later which brought the entire grant for the expedition up to £1,500.[97]

The most animated controversy occured in 1756 over a bill granting £30,000 for the second Crown Point campaign. In this bill the assembly named certain officers, including agents to go to Albany to look after the disbursement of their money. The

---

[93] *N. H. Prov. Pap.*, vi, various messages to the governor.

[94] *Ibid.*, 319. "It being uncertain whether the Assembly will pay the Troops for any longer time than their Grants extended to, I think it proper that you give orders for dismissing both the Troops posted on Merrimack and those on Connecticut River, unless they are willing to remain at the mercy of the Assembly, which I cannot advise to." Gov. Wentworth to Col. Blanchard, Nov. 3, 1754.

[95] *Ibid.*, 361.

[96] *Ibid.*, 409.

[97] *Ibid.*, 439-441. Report of Secretary Atkinson.

council approved the bill,[98] but the governor at first refused his assent. Asserting that it was an encroachment upon the "Prerogative of the Crown," the governor asked that the bill be altered, but the assembly denied the charge and refused to amend it.[99] The governor showed them his instructions from England expressly forbidding him to sign such a bill,[100] but in the end he was forced to break his instructions and sign it.[1] Wentworth's position was not an easy one. On this and other occasions he showed a desire to be fair, but his instructions were explicit and he felt bound to obey them. The assembly cared little about the war and had nothing to lose by delay, but the members knew that the governor would be discredited in England if he should fail to secure aid from his province. They saw the advantage of their position and made the most of it. They were not the only assembly that denied the binding force of royal instructions and welcomed an opportunity to nullify them.

III. THE MIDDLE COLONIES

NEW YORK

New York was already the scene of discord before war with the French began. Governor Clinton, a firm believer in prerogative, had for some time been urging the home government to curb the independent tendencies of the assembly.

In April, 1751, the Board of Trade made an elaborate report to the Privy Council on conditions in New York and accompanied it with a mass of evidence to prove that the assembly had been disregarding royal instructions and usurping powers that did not belong to them. The principal charges were that the assembly had refused to grant permanent salaries to royal officials, and had taken the control of money disbursements

[98] *N. H. Prov. Pap.*, vi, 506-508.

[99] *Ibid.*, 509-511.

[100] *Ibid.*, 517. He added, ". . . . if I could dispense with the King's Instructions, the Royal Prerogative the Powers Authorities and Reservations of the Crown, with as much ease as you do in the House, I should find no difficulty to persuade myself to consent to your Bill."

[1] *Ibid.*, 520.

entirely into their own hands. In this report Halifax and his
colleagues stated very clearly what they considered the panacea
for colonial disorders.

> ''There is nothing so essencially necessary to the preservation of His
> Maj^{ty's} Govern^t in the American provinces, as the careful and strict
> maintenance of the just prerogative, which is the only means by which
> those Colonies can be kept dependent on the mouther Country, or the Gov-
> ernors themselves representing the Crown, maintain any power over their
> Assemblies, or any agreement with them.
>
> ''No Govr departed from the prerogative in one instance, but he raised
> in the Assembly a confidence to attack it in another, which as constantly
> brings on contests, which again create animosities, which in the end obstruct
> all Parts of Govern^t.''[2]

It was certainly true that in New York and other colonies
the assemblies had assumed executive powers. It was equally
true that they made much of precedent in justifying their conduct. On the other hand, ''prerogative'' was a most indefinite
and mysterious thing, which in the hands of an unscrupulous
executive might easily be used to paralyze legitimate legislative
functions.

About the same time as the above report the Board of Trade
advised that a new governor be appointed and given stricter
instructions,[3] but this was not done until two years later. In
1753 Sir Danvers Osborne, brother-in-law of Halifax, was
appointed and armed with instructions which were prepared
by Halifax, Townshend, and Oswald.[4]

The instructions[5] were prefaced with the assertion that in
New York ''the peace and tranquility of the said province has
been disturbed; order and government subverted; and our royal
prerogative and authority trampled upon, and invaded in a
most unwarrantable and illegal manner.''

After specifying some of the ''unwarrantable proceedings''
of the assembly, the governor was instructed to re-establish good

---

[2] *N. Y. Col. Hist. Docs.*, vi, 614.

[3] Bancroft, *History of the United States*, ed. 22, iv, 5.

[4] *N. Y. Col. Hist. Docs.*, vi, 788-791.

[5] Dated Aug. 13, 1753. Extracts given in *Gentleman's Magazine* for
Feb., 1754, xxiv, 65.

order by requiring a permanent salary for crown officials, and also that all money voted should be spent by warrant of the governor approved by the council, and not otherwise. The assembly, however, were to have the privilege of examining the accounts of the money spent.[6]

Osborne found that instructions were more easily issued than enforced. Before he announced the new requirements he was informed by the city council that they would not "brook any infringement of their inestimable liberties, civil or religious." His own council informed him that the assembly would never obey the new instructions. But Osborne did not live to put them to the test. Already melancholy on account of Lady Osborne's death, he hanged himself on the night following this discouraging news from his council.[7]

The government now devolved upon DeLancey, who succeeded in effecting a compromise for the time being. The assembly declared that they would never grant permanent salaries no matter how many times they might be dissolved, but consented to yield some of the executive powers which they had exercised.[8] They sent an address to the king asserting that they had been "most falsely and maliciously represented" by the Board of Trade. As Osborne's instructions had been based on these representations, the Board of Trade submitted another report to the king, April 4, 1754, in which they reiterated the charges. During the previous war, they said, when the governor had been obliged to assent to unjust laws or go without funds, the assembly had "taken to themselves not only the management and disposal of such publick money but have also wrested from your Majesty's Governor the nomination of all officers of Government the custody and direction of the publick military stores, the mustering and direction of troops raised for your

---

[6] Bancroft erroneously states that "the Assembly should never be allowed to examine accounts." (iv, 104; also his "Last Revision," ii, 376.)

[7] Bancroft, iv, 104; *N. Y. Col. Hist. Docs.*, vi, 833.

[8] *N. Y. Col. Hist. Docs.*, vi, 820. DeLancey to Board of Trade, Jan. 3, 1754.

Majesty's service, and in short almost every other part of executive Government.''[9]

This brief statement, although applied to New York only, covers generally the demands made by nearly every colony which controlled only the legislative branch of government. Whenever the assemblies were asked for money they usually insisted on dictating the manner of its disbursement. They did not ask simply that money voted for a specific purpose should not be used for other things. This would have been legitimate and praiseworthy. They insisted that all money granted should be placed in the hands of a committee appointed by themselves and under their control. Under this arrangement the governor had to apply to the committee for funds to meet the smallest expenditures, and the committee in turn could do nothing without the consent of the assembly. Executive functions of government were made subject to the caprice of the legislative body.

Early in 1754 the New York assembly voted £1,000 to provision two companies which the king had ordered to be sent from New York to Virginia. While technically complying with the king's command, they had drawn the bill in such a way that the council could not concur without violating their instructions. They informed the council that unless the bill should pass without change not ''a farthing'' would be granted.[10] When Lieutenant-Governor DeLancey reported this matter to the Board of Trade he criticised both houses for their obstinacy, and he blamed the council especially for not yielding on such an important occasion.[11] But this half defense of the assembly signifies little, for DeLancey at this time was trying to win the good will of that body. In this he succeeded, and soon used his influence over the assembly to compel Governor Hardy to sign private money bills in DeLancey's favor by attaching them to bills for

[9] *N. Y. Col. Hist. Docs.*, vi, 831-832.

[10] *Ibid.*, vi, 834; *Pa. Arch.*, ser. 2, vi, 183.

[11] *N. Y. Col. Hist. Docs.*, vi, 838.

defense.[12] The Board of Trade supported the council in its refusal to disobey instructions. The assembly, not wishing to ignore the king's command entirely, voted £5,000 to aid Virginia, but made it payable to DeLancey, thus depriving the governor of any control over the money.[13] On account of this trouble and consequent delay the New York companies did not reach Virginia until the middle of June. The companies were incomplete, of poor quality, and poorly equipped.[14]

When money was needed there were certain points on which the two houses could not agree. The assembly endeavored to retain absolute control of disbursements. When issuing bills of credit they refused to comply with royal instructions, which required a clause suspending operation of the law until the king's approval could be secured. The instructions limited bills of credit to a term of five years, but the assembly persisted in issuing them for a longer time.

Disputes over these questions occurred in all royal and proprietary colonies. Controversies of this character led the colonists to formulate their political theories, to assert their "rights," and to attempt to find a constitutional basis for those "rights."

In the spring of 1755 the assembly of New York receded from their former position to the extent of permitting the council and the commander-in-chief to act with them in the management and disbursement of money, but they still refused to insert a suspending clause in their bills for issuing paper money.[15] After they had forced the governor to sign a bill without such a clause,

---

[12] The assembly passed a bill for raising troops to serve in the Crown Point expedition and for frontier defense. The term of service was limited to forty days. Another bill was passed authorizing the payment to DeLancey of £3,787, 16s, for services, not specified. The governor was told that if he would consent to the latter he might fix the term of service in the former to suit himself. Under the circumstances he signed both bills. *Coll. Mass. Hist. Soc.*, ser. 1, vii, 144-145.

[13] *N. Y. Col. Hist. Docs.*, vi, 90.

[14] *Dinwiddie Papers*, i, 245.

[15] Having secured the passage of a bill for £45,000 with the suspending clause omitted, they then voted 800 men for the war, and, on hearing of Braddock's defeat, 400 more. *N. Y. Col. Hist. Docs.*, vi, 940, 989; *Corresp. of Gov. Sharpe*, i, 170.

they then enacted a militia law which Hardy pronounced to be
not only the best but the only effective law of the kind in the
colonies at that time.[16] The records of other colonies seem to
bear out this statement. Some of them for a long time refused
to pass a militia law of any kind.

Governor Hardy soon had reason to see the force of what the
Board of Trade had said concerning precedent. Having yielded
once in the paper money controversy he was obliged to do so
again. In 1756 the assembly voted £40,000 in bills of credit for
war purposes. Hardy endeavored to have the bills made payable
within five years but was finally obliged to disregard his instructions and sign the bill as it was presented to him.[17]

Having preserved the most vital of their constitutional
"rights," the members of the assembly were quite generous with
both men and money in succeeding years. In 1759 they raised
£150,000 by loan for the king's service and paid it all within a
year.[18] The ability of the assembly to repay such a large amount
in so short a time indicates that its opposition to the five-year
limit on bills of credit was not well grounded, for the opposition
had been based on the inability of the colony to cancel its bills
within five years.

NEW JERSEY

In New Jersey there was less friction than in any of the other
middle colonies. Here we have the very unusual record of two
governors—one in the early part and another toward the close
of the war—speaking in high terms of the loyalty of their assemblies. Governor Belcher wrote to Richard Partridge, December
20, 1755, that "N. Jersey is well alive & exerts to the Honor &
Interest of their King & Country & the whole Legislature
(Govr, Council, & Assembly) are in great harmony among themselves." On July 7, 1761, the assembly complimented Governor
Boone on his administration and expressed a willingness to vote

---

[16] *N. Y. Col. Hist. Docs.*, vii, 3. Hardy to Board of Trade, Jan. 16, 1756.
[17] *Ibid.*, 37.
[18] *Ibid.*, 343, 395, 430.

all necessary funds.   On July 28, Boone praised the assembly
very highly in a letter to the Board of Trade.[19]

In the summer of 1754, £15,000 was granted by the assembly
to finance Colonel Schuyler in his operations in New York, and
later five hundred men were raised in New Jersey to go with
him to serve under General Shirley in the proposed attack on
Niagara.[20]

The records show that New Jersey was far less jealous of her
neighbors than most of the other colonies, and the assembly was
usually willing to permit the troops to serve wherever the commanding general needed them.   The troops sent to Niagara had
been originally intended for Crown Point,[21] and there was no
objection to having the governor send troops to Pennsylvania at
a time when the assembly of that province would do nothing for
their own defense.[22]   Their only protest was a reasonable one—
that troops raised and paid by New Jersey should be employed
in her defense unless there should be greater need of them elsewhere.[23]   Their attitude was all the more commendable because
their own province was almost entirely without means of
defense.[24]

Considering the size and resources of the colony, the assembly
was generous with money.   During one period of less than two
years £140,000 in proclamation money was granted for war
purposes.[25]

About the only thing that seriously disturbed the harmony
in New Jersey was a controversy over the issuing of paper
money.   In this matter members of the assembly for a time
asserted their ''rights'' as defiantly as the legislators of any
other colony.   As in other colonies they took advantage of the
financial needs of the executive and forced through issues of

---

[19] *N. J. Arch.*, ser. 1, ix, 287, 299.

[20] *N. J. Arch.*, ser. 1, viii, part 2, 11; *Pa. Arch., 1748-56*, ii, 312.

[21] *Pa. Arch.*, ser. 2, vi, 245, et seq.

[22] *Pa. Arch., 1748-56*, ii, 481.

[23] *N. J. Arch.*, ser. 1, viii, part 2, 194.

[24] *Ibid.*, Belcher to Board of Trade.

[25] *Ibid.*, ix, 167.   Governor Bernard to Pitt, March 20, 1759.

paper by joining grants for the war with those for paying old debts. Such a bill was passed in November of 1754. It provided for the emission of £70,000 in bills of credit, only £10,000 of which was for the king's service, the remainder to be used for sinking old bills. This money was made a legal tender although the Board of Trade had opposed such a measure on former occasions. When the Board now refused its assent to the present issue the assembly followed the example set by Pennsylvania and Maryland. It sent a petition to the king asking his permission to emit legal tender paper, and flatly refused to vote any assistance until the king's will should be ascertained.[26] No definite settlement seems to have been reached at this time but apparently the governor yielded to the terms of the assembly, for similar laws were passed from time to time without difficulty until 1757, when the governor again objected to the legal tender clause. Once more the assembly petitioned the king. Its petition was considered by the Board of Trade which reported adversely in November of that year.[27]

In 1758 Bernard, who was then governor, sided with the assembly and asked the Board of Trade for permission to sign bills for issuing legal tender paper. He urged that there was now no legal tender money except British gold and silver, of which there was practically none in the colony. The people, he said, carried on considerable trade with Pennsylvania and New York and it was therefore necessary that the only money they possessed should be made a legal tender. Whether this was sound reasoning or not, the Board of Trade accepted it and recommended that the governor be instructed to sign the bills. Both king and Privy Council acquiesced.[28] The usual good conduct and public spirit of the colony no doubt contributed to this amicable settlement.

Barring this dispute over paper money the assembly manifested a desire to do all that the colony was able to do for the

---

[26] *N. J. Arch.*, ser. 1, viii, part 2, 36 et seq., 152; *Pa. Arch., 1748-56,* ii, 269.

[27] *N. J. Arch.*, ser. 1, ix, 11-14, 34-38.

[28] *Ibid.*, 131-139, 147-148, 154-158.

common cause. There is little evidence of those belligerent characteristics so common in the neighboring colonies. On most occasions they possessed, as Governor Morris of Pennsylvania said in 1755, "a due regard both to the rights of Governm^t and the Libertys of the people.[29]

PENNSYLVANIA

Pennsylvania offers the most interesting field for a study of the contest between the legislative and executive branches of government. This contest was already in progress when hostilities with the French began, and it continued practically unabated throughout the war period.

In crown colonies there were but two opposing interests to harmonize—those of the people, represented by the assembly; and those of the crown, represented by the governor. In a proprietary colony like Pennsylvania still another factor was added to complicate matters, for the interests of the proprietor were usually entirely personal and did not harmonize with the welfare of either of the other parties concerned. The Quaker, also, with his aversion to war and his fearless—often arbitrary—disposition, furnished his own peculiar contribution to the difficult task of those whose duty it was to defend the colonies from the attacks of the enemy.

In no other colony was obstinacy carried to such an extreme on either side; nowhere else was there such open defiance of all authority not derived directly from the people. In their verbal contests with their governors succeeding assemblies of Pennsylvania promulgated, more clearly than the assembly of any other colony, the colonial opinion of their relation to the mother country, and what they considered to be the rights and duties on either side. During this war their criticisms were aimed primarily at the validity of proprietary instructions; but in discussing these the assembly covered generally the entire field of colonial government; the rights, duties, and limitations of

---

[29] *Pa. Arch., 1748-65,* ii, 501. Morris to Belcher, Nov. 17, 1775.

crown, Parliament, and colonies. As mentioned elsewhere, nearly
every argument used to combat the Stamp Act and those which
followed it may be found in these discussions of the Pennsylvania assembly. Franklin was a member of the assembly before
his departure for England. He admits being the "penman"[30]
of some of the addresses of the assembly and he was usually
credited with supplying the arguments on constitutional questions. His hatred of proprietary rule was very pronounced and
he was ever ready to use his influence to bring about its overthrow. In the *Historical Review of Pennsylvania,* which was
probably inspired by Franklin and certainly endorsed by him,
proprietary government is described as one with an "assuming
landlord, strongly disposed to convert free tenants into abject
vassals, and to reap what he did not sow, countenanced and
abetted by a few desperate and designing dependents, on the
one side; and on the other, all who have sense enough to know
their rights, and spirit enough to defend them, combined as one
man against the said landlord, and his encroachments."[31] The
assembly denied that the proprietors had the right to obstruct
legislation by rigid instructions to the governor. All the "public
quarrels," said Franklin, were caused by the Penns, who, "with
incredible meanness, instructed their deputies to pass no act for
levying the necessary taxes, unless their vast estates were in the
same act expressly exonerated; and they had even taken the
bonds of these deputies to observe such instructions."[32]

Franklin's hatred for the proprietors is apparent in all his

---

[30] *Works,* i, 215. In another place he wrote: "I was put on every committee for answering his (Morris) speeches and messages, and by the committees always desired to make the drafts. Our answers, as well as his
messages, were often tart, and sometimes indecently abusive." pp. 179-180.

[31] Franklin, *Works,* iii, 113; i, 180-181.

[32] ". . . . every proprietary governor . . . . has two masters, one who
gives him his commission, and one who gives him his pay; that he is on his
good behavior to both; that. if he does not fulfill with rigor every proprietary command, however injurious to the province or offensive to the assembly, he is recalled; that if he does not gratify the assembly in what they
think they have a right to claim, he is certain to live in perpetual broils,
though uncertain whether he shall be able to live at all; and that, upon the
whole, to be a governor upon such terms is to be the most wretched thing
alive." Franklin, *Works,* iii, 187.

writings. He seemed, however, to have some sympathy for their governors whose duty it was, as pointed out by the author of the *Historical Review,* to serve two masters.[33] During the most heated quarrels Franklin kept up a personal friendship with the governors.

It is evident that one at least of the leaders of the opponents of the proprietors was not averse to using money for the purpose of nullifying proprietary instructions when resistance did not have the desired effect. In the *Historical Review* the author[34] pointed to Sir William Keith as one of the best and wisest governors, who, having the same instructions as others, hinted to the assembly that "in case they would pay him well, he would serve them well." Keith was recalled by the proprietors, and the author regretted that the assembly did not "set a lustre on his dismission, by accompanying it with all the *doucers* in the power of the province to have heaped upon him, that other governors might have thought it worth their while to proceed on his plan." He used the example of Keith's administration to show that Pennsylvania "when well governed, is easily governed." *Well governed* in his opinion seems to have meant an all-powerful assembly and a hireling governor. In another place the author frankly stated that "the subjects' money is never so well disposed of as in the maintenance of order and tranquility, and the purchase of good laws; for which felicities Keith's administration was deservedly memorable."[35] It was to a naturally stubborn assembly, led by men who openly advocated buying or crushing any governor who opposed them, that the British government must look for men and supplies to carry on the war.

It was only in times of war and of extraordinary expense

[33] Franklin, *Works,* 187-193.

[34] This *Review* was published by Franklin (*Works,* i, 215) and it was generally supposed that he wrote it, but he afterwards denied the authorship (*Works,* vii, 208). At any rate, he endorsed it and published it to aid his cause. Fisher says that it was written by Franklin's son. *Colony and Commonwealth,* 216.

[35] Franklin, *Works,* iii, 187-193.

that the question of taxing proprietary estates became an important issue, for ordinary expenses of government were derived
from excises and interest on bills of credit loaned out. A land
tax was not levied.[36] During the previous war a land tax had
become necessary. The assembly insisted on taxing the proprietary estates for public purposes whenever other lands were
taxed, but the governor under instructions from the proprietors
had refused to pass bills for that purpose. In 1753, the assembly
appealed from the governor to the proprietors and were censured by the Penns who asserted that the assembly had raised
the claim purely as an election cry to please the people. The
Penns maintained that they were "under no greater obligation
to contribute to the Public Charges than the Chief Governor
of another Colony," and referred to a former opinion of the
Board of Trade which sustained them in this contention.[37] But
neither the proprietors nor the Board of Trade were able to
convince the assembly that the Penns in their capacity of property owners should not contribute to the defense of that property,
simply because they happened also to be proprietors of the
province. Not being convinced the assembly insisted on taxing
proprietary estates whenever other lands were taxed for purposes of defense.

The constitutional controversy in Pennsylvania is more easily
understood after a brief examination of the documents on which
the claims of the assembly were based.

The author of the *Historical Review* states in his opening
chapter that the constitution of Pennsylvania is derived from
three sources: "the *birthright* of every British subject," the
royal charter granted to Penn, and the charter of privileges
granted by Penn to the inhabitants of the colony in 1701.[38]
This puts in concise form the oft-repeated declarations of the

---

[36] Franklin, *Works,* i, 232.

[37] Thomas and Richard Penn to House of Rep., *Pa. Arch., 1748-56,* ii,
109. In 1750 the Penns told the assembly that they did not "conceive
themselves under any obligation to contribute to Indian or any other publick Expenses." *Pa. Col. Rec.,* v, 546.

[38] Franklin, *Works,* iii, 116.

assembly. The last two are more tangible than the first and
were used whenever they would answer the purpose, but the
first was an important asset to have in reserve and all the more
valuable because of its indefinite character. For example, the
same author after asserting that the proprietors are bound by
the terms of the charter, points out that even the "crown is
limited in all its acts and grants by the fundamentals of the
constitution and can not . . . . establish any colony upon, or
contract it within a narrower scale, than the subject is entitled
to by the Great Charter of England."[39] Here again the author
simply states a claim often used to good advantage by the assembly. The royal charter and the charter privileges bound the
proprietor in matters covered by them and were good as far as
they went, but the rights of the subject transcended both, and
both were void wherever they abridged the privileges included
in the "birthright of Englishmen." The inconsistency of this
claim with the opinion held generally in the colonies, that their
only connection with England was through the crown, seems
never to have dawned upon those who made it.

The parts of the royal charter most frequently called in
question were those which related to the enactment of laws and
to the royal veto. The charter states in a general way that with
the assent of the freemen Penn, his heirs, and their deputies,
may enact all necessary laws. The assembly held that the charter
thus gave the deputies full power to sign laws regardless of
proprietary instructions, and that such instructions were indeed
a violation of the charter. It is worthy to note that in many of
their discussions they do not regard proprietary instructions in
the light of a veto, but represent the proprietor as attempting
to legislate by instructions thereby violating the charter.

The provision made in the charter for the royal veto was
roundabout and burdensome. It required that a transcript of all
laws passed in the province must be sent to England within five
years after their passage. If not vetoed by the king or Privy

---

[39] Franklin, *Works*, iii, 121.

Council within six months after reaching England the laws were to be valid and binding. It will be seen at once that this elastic provision if rigorously enforced might work real hardship in the colony. A law went into effect at once in the colony and if vetoed several years after its passage, making business transacted under it illegal, much damage might result. There is evidence that the Board of Trade sometimes hesitated to recommend a veto provided the colony would agree to refrain from passing such a law in future.

In a law involving the finances of the colony such as an act for the emission of paper money it would seem that a clause suspending its operation until the king's approval could be secured would be preferable to a veto after the money had been put in circulation. But the assembly took a different view of the matter and considered a suspending clause an oppressive requirement. Some historians hold the same view. Fisher in his eulogy on the assembly[40] goes so far as to assert that the incorporation of a suspending clause "would have been surrendering one of the colony's most important rights."

In the charter of liberties granted by Penn in 1701 the assembly found other safeguards of their liberties. This document gave the assembly the privilege of initiating laws which it did not possess under the earlier frames of government, but it also in some respects enlarged the powers of the proprietor. It has been asserted [41] that this charter greatly enlarged Penn's veto powers, but aside from giving him greater control over council little change seems to have been made by the document itself. The style of the enacting clause in either case might be interpreted to give Penn the right to veto laws.

The charter of privileges permitted the assembly to "sit upon their own Adjournments." This was a wholesome concession to popular government and in ordinary times seems to

---

[40] Fisher, *Pennsylvania Colony and Commonwealth*, 148.

[41] *Historical Review of Pennsylvania*, in Franklin, *Works*, iii, 157. The author says: "Instead of having but three voices in seventy-two, he was left single in the executive, and at liberty to restrain the legislative by refusing his assent to their bills whenever he thought fit."

have caused little discord, but in a period of intense feeling like the one under consideration the assembly abused this privilege for the purpose of annoying and defeating the governor. Instances of this will appear in the following pages.

From the beginning of the war the assembly determined to keep control of all funds voted for defense. Early in 1754 they voted £5,000 for war purposes, but instead of putting it at the disposal of the executive they placed it in the hands of five of their own members.[42] In April (1754) the governor called a special session to consider matters of defense as well as the advisability of sending representatives to the Albany convention. Letters on the needs of the colonies from several governors were read and aid was asked for General Shirley in his northern campaigns. On the abstract question of granting a sum of money for the king's service the assembly voted by a small majority (18 to 16) in the affirmative, but when it came to voting any definite sum—from £20,000 down to £5,000—they defeated each proposal by a large majority. The only thing they would consent to do was to grant £500 to be sent as a present to the Indians, after which they adjourned for a month, despite the governor's protest, for the purpose of consulting their constituents.[43]

They met again in May and framed a bill which they knew the governor could not approve, because it embodied the features which were forbidden by his instructions. The bill provided for the emission of £30,000 in bills of credit to be paid within ten years, although the British government had fixed five years as the limit for such bills. The governor asked them to shorten the time to four years but they refused to alter it. In another respect they violated the rules adopted for the colonies. Of the £30,000 only £10,000 was for the king; the remainder was to be used for the redemption of old bills. The governor was obliged to accept the grant with the attached rider or go without the £10,000. In their address to the governor the assembly emphatically asserted that "the Representatives of the

---

[42] *Pa. Arch.*, *1748-56*, ii, 114-115. Hamilton to Sharpe, Jan. 7, 1754.

[43] *Ibid.*, 235; *Pa. Col. Rec.*, vii, 25-26.

People have an Undoubted Right to judge and determine not only the Sum to be raised for Use of the Crown, but the Manner of raising it.''[44]   When the expected veto came they adjourned until August without voting a shilling for the common defense. Before adjourning the question of colonial union was discussed, and the members of the assembly showed the independent spirit of the colony by denying the binding force of any such union.[45] In the August session, after several refusals to grant funds, they drew a bill for granting £3,500 similar to the one that had been vetoed in May.[46]   The governor of course was compelled by his instructions to veto this also, and the question of supplies and consideration of the Albany plan of union were postponed to the next session, when the new governor, Morris, would have arrived.

Fisher,[47] who is ever ready to eulogize the assembly, absolves that body from all blame in the extreme position to which they adhered.   He makes the unqualified assertion that ''It was not the Pennsylvania Assembly that was to blame, but her governor, who by the necessity of a war supply wished to force the colony to yield its rights established by the struggles of over seventy years.''   He attributes adverse criticism of their conduct to ignorance and superficial investigation on the part of other historians.   While the selfishness of the proprietors stands out in bold relief, and the governors in many cases were overzealous in the interests of their masters, he who would prove the assembly faultless and unselfish in all things should not examine too closely the records of their proceedings.

If Governor Morris had hopes of succeeding where Hamilton had failed he was soon to be undeceived.   Before he had been in the colony long he had reason to appreciate the feeling of Governor Shirley of Massachusetts who wrote him about this

[44] *Pa. Col. Rec.*, vi, 39-40.

[45] *Ibid.*, 45.

[46] *Pa. Arch., 1748-56,* ii, 189, 235, 236.   This provided for issuing £35,000 in bills of credit—£15,000 for military purposes, and the remainder for cancelling old bills.

[47] Fisher, 147, 148.

time "I have no leaf in my books for managing a Quaker Assembly." The only remedy which Shirley could suggest was
union and control "by Act of Parliam^t, as soon as possible."[48]
Morris told Franklin[49] that he "loved disputing." If this was
true his administration must have afforded him real pleasure.
When he met the assembly in December he encountered the same
difficulties that had marked the administration of Hamilton. He
urged the need of money for defense and the assembly sent him
a bill for striking £40,000 in bills of credit—half for the king's
use to be applied as the governor saw fit, the other half to be
controlled by the assembly. All was to be sunk by an excise to
run for twelve years, although such issues were limited by an
act of Parliament to five years. Alleging this and the omis-
sion of a suspending clause as reasons, Morris refused to sign
the bill and the assembly refused to vote funds on any other
terms. His real reason for vetoing the bill, he told Penn, was
that it gave the assembly control of half of the money, but he
thought it better to use all possible objections.[50] He finally
agreed to sign a bill without a suspending clause if they would
reduce the term to five years. While the bill was being passed
back and forth many times between governor and assembly—
each trying to exhaust the other into compliance—the latter
gave an opinion of their rights as Englishmen which could hardly
be surpassed during the Revolutionary struggle. They told the
governor that in a small matter they might yield, "yet in this
Case our all is concerned, and if we should not act becoming
the Rights as Englishmen entitle us to, we might appear un-
worthy the Regard we have already experienced and have good
Reason to hope for hereafter from a British Parliament." The
people, they said, "are convinced they ought not to be governed
by Proprietary Instructions in Opposition to their Charter,
which is, in our Opinion, the Foundation and Sanction of our

[48] *Pa. Arch., 1748-56,* ii, 181.

[49] Franklin, *Works,* i, 179.

[50] Letters to Penn, Robinson, and Sharpe, *Pa. Arch., 1748-56,* ii, 216,
221, 224, 237.

Civil and Religious Liberties; and especially if these Instructions must be secreted from them, and by that Means the whole
country left without any known Rule of their Conduct.'"[51]
From an American standpoint this is good constitutional doctrine, but if all of their claims had been conceded it would have
to be admitted that the charter had given them virtual independence, which of course was not the case.

Having prepared an appeal to the king, the assembly resolved
to borrow £5,000 on their own credit to be spent by themselves
for defense. They then adjourned abruptly without the governor's knowledge or consent.[52] Morris despaired of coming to
any agreement with men who were willing to let their own
province be overrun by the enemy[53] while they indulged in dis-
sertations on the force of royal and proprietary instructions. It
is strange, however, that it seems never to have occurred to the
governor that those who instructed him might also be somewhat
culpable if the enemy were given a free field for operations in
order that they might preserve all of their alleged privileges
intact and their rent-roll undiminished. He saw only the
obstinacy of the colonists, and he hoped that Parliament would
unite them and put things on "such a footing as to leave no room
for future contests between governors and assemblies." Their
inactivity, he said, had already put the home government to
"thinking."[54]

---

[51] *Pa. Col. Rec.*, vi, 191 et seq., 207, 229.

[52] *Ibid.*, 295. Morris to Dinwiddie.

[53] *Pa. Arch., 1748-56*, ii, 231. Morris to Shirley, Dec. 29, 1754. He
wrote to Dinwiddie, Jan. 7, 1755, ". . . . surely there never was a set of
people in the world, so stupidly infatuated, or so blind to their country's
danger as the Assemblys of these Colonys have been upon the present
occasion, but if any of 'em are entitled to stand foremost upon the infatuated List, it is the people of this province, who are rich, flourishing and
numerous, and not only decline taking up arms upon this occasion, but
even refuse to offer the assistance or supply the articles expected from
them by the Crown" . . . . "I nave no expectations from a set of men
that are, or pretend to be, principal'd against defending themselves or
their Country, & who, at such a time as this, chuse to enter into a dispute
concerning the force of the King's Instructions, and pursuing measures
rather calculated to aggrandize their own power, than to Promote the public
service." *Ibid.*, 226, 227.

[54] *Ibid.*, 227. Morris to Dinwiddie.

Morris did not, perhaps, state the entire truth when he informed Sir Thomas Robinson that the assembly had "no other design but to furnish a pretence for not acting as his Majesty's service and the safety of the country required," but it was true as he said in the same letter, that "Royal & Proprietary Instructions were (are) by no means new things in this Government, and if they had been destructive of the Libertys of the people, they might have been complained of in a time of less danger."[55] He had still better ground for asserting that "if a house of Assembly by their own Authority, without the consent or Approbation of a Govr, can borrow and dispose of money as they think proper," they could easily use this method to overthrow their dependence upon the crown.[56] The real truth seems to be that the assembly and their constituents were actuated not so much by a wish to shirk entirely their duty to the king as by the desire to show that proprietary government was detrimental to the interests of both king and subjects. This they hoped to do by maintaining that arbitrary instructions alone prevented them from assisting the king in the defense of his colonial possessions. They denied that the proprietor had authority to issue such instructions, and for that reason the governor was not bound to obey them. Such instructions, they said, were "distructive of their Libertys and infractions of their charter."[57] It is evident also that they hoped by standing firm to force an acknowledgment of new "rights" which they could never hope to secure in times of peace.

Thomas Penn fully sustained the governor as a matter of course and expressed deep disappointment because the people for whom his family had done so much were now trying in every way to injure them.[58] But if Penn deceived himself with respect to the gratitude owed him by the colonists, he could hardly hope

---

[55] Still it should be remembered that a land tax, including a tax on proprietary estates which caused the present dispute, became an important issue only in times of war or other heavy expense.

[56] *Pa. Arch., 1748-56,* ii, 249-250.

[57] *Ibid.*

[58] *Ibid.,* 252-253.

to deceive others. Whatever the motives were that had caused the founder of the colony to grant quite liberal privileges to the settlers, there is no evidence to indicate that the present proprietors considered the interests of the people farther than their ability to afford an income to themselves.

Penn wrote that "it is not believed here that they ever intended to give a shilling," and that he saw little hope of getting money for defense so long as people who scruple to bear arms were permitted to sit in the assembly.[59]

To induce the assembly to yield, General Braddock sent a special letter for the governor to lay before them. He pointed out that the success of the French was due to the want of a proper union and lack of support in the British colonies; that Pennsylvania was amply able to support a campaign in which she was so directly interested; and that she ought not to take advantage of the common danger for the purpose of making encroachments on the king's prerogative.[60] A similar letter from Lord Halifax was shown them and Morris had hopes that the two would "make a Proper Impression," but so little were they heeded that the assembly refused to vote new supplies except on the same inadmissible terms,[61] and the commissioners in charge of the £5,000 above mentioned refused even to advance a small sum to the governor for the purpose of returning deserters. Their excuse was that their instructions from the assembly did not cover that point.[62] It had at last reached a point where the governor was forced to ask a committee of the assembly for funds to cover the smallest items of ⁕expense, and even these humiliating requests were often denied.

The people in general showed the same attitude as the mem-

---

[59] *Pa. Arch., 1748-56,* ii, 252, 257.

[60] *Pa. Col. Rec.,* vi, 332.

[61] They granted £25,000 to the king, only £5,000 of which was put at this disposal of Braddock. The remainder was to be used by the assembly as *they* saw fit. When the governor refused to pass the bill the assembly demanded that it be returned to them, but the governor kept it that he might send it to the king for the purpose of exposing the conduct of the assembly. *Pa. Col. Rec.,* vi, 339, 353, 386, 389.

[62] *Pa. Arch., 1748-56,* ii, 271, 272.

bers of the assembly. Their indifference if not hostility to British interests is shown by their refusal to furnish conveyances to British troops, even for pay, and by their trading with the French and Indians in powder and other supplies.[63] Franklin at last secured authority from Braddock to advertise for conveyances and urged the people to respond. He pointed out that in this way they might procure a supply of much needed specie. He warned them also that the king's officers were much exasperated with the colony and would take what they needed if they could not buy or hire it.[64] Fear and the influence of Franklin secured some assistance from both the people and the assembly committee. While they were not so "determined to assist the war," as Fisher[65] represents them to have been, this and their aid in connection with the military road seems to have appeased the wrath of Braddock and elicited his commendation.[66]

In June (1755) the assembly scored a victory by forcing the governor to pass a bill embodying some of the objectionable features. Regardless of previous vetoes they presented a bill for granting £25,000—£15,000 for war purposes, and £10,000 for sinking old bills of credit. They accompanied it with a copy of a similar law which had been approved in England. Yielding to financial pressure the governor signed the bill after a futile attempt to have it amended.[67]

Braddock's defeat in July caused general excitement in the colonies and nearly all of them responded to new requests for supplies with more promptness than usual. On August 1, the Pennsylvania assembly voted £50,000, but knowing the governor's instructions as they did, it is not at all probable that they had any expectation that the grant would be accepted, because of the terms on which it was offered. The amount was to be raised

[63] On May 4, 1755, Braddock ordered Morris to put a stop to this trade. If it were not stopped, he would take in hand himself. *Pa. Arch., 1748-56,* ii, 299.

[64] *Ibid.,* 294.

[65] *Pennsylvania Colony and Commonwealth,* 155.

[66] *Diary of Daniel Fisher,* in *Pa. Mag. of Hist.,* xvii, 272.

[67] *Pa. Col. Rec.,* vi, 437-447.

by a tax on all estates, including those of the proprietors, and the discussion which now arose over this question was one of the most acrimonious of the war period. The addresses of the assembly were written by Franklin, so Governor Morris said, and according to the former's own writings the statement is no doubt true. Franklin covered in considerable detail the rights and duties of the people as well as their relation to both proprietor and king. The discussion is too long and technical to be treated in full, but the main points will be considered.

The governor based his objections to the bill mainly on three grounds. First, his instructions. Second, the proprietors from the very nature of things should not be taxed. Third, former laws had exempted these estates and established a precedent. The assembly refuted these arguments and gave many reasons why the estates should be taxed. The assembly claimed it as a right to have all money bills accepted or rejected as a whole—without amendment. They had waived this right at times, they said, but still possessed it. Whence they acquired the right they do not make clear. It was probably a derivative of the "birth-right of Englishmen," for it is not guaranteed by either of the charters on which they based so many of their claims. Propriet-ary instructions, in their opinion, could be no valid excuse for the governor's refusal to sign such bills. The lieutenant-gov-ernor,[68] they said, had been given full power to act by the royal charter, therefore proprietary instructions could not take away this right.[69] They maintained that general proprietary exemp-tions did not apply in the case of a land tax; the proprietor was taxed as a landholder, not as proprietor or governor. They cited

---

[68] It should be remembered that the proprietor was also governor. His representative in Pennsylvania although usually called governor was technic-ally only lieutenant-governor.

[69] The charter is so worded, but it is doubtful that it was the intention to make the deputy independent of his chief or to give him power to enact laws in opposition to the wishes of the latter. The charter reads: ". . . . Doe grant free, full and absolute power, . . . to him and his heirs, and his and their Deputies, and Lieutenants, . . . to ordeyne, make, Enact and . . . . to publish any Laws whatsoever, for the raising of money for the publick use of the said province, or for any other End apperteyning either to the publick state, peace, or safety of the said Countrey."

evidence to show that the king himself was subject to a tax on his lands. The proprietor could not claim more than the king. Far from being entitled to exemptions the assembly asserted that the proprietor had no right to the fees and licenses which had been allowed him for the purpose of paying the lieutenant-governor's salary. The founder of the colony had been permitted to collect quit-rents in lieu of a salary as governor. When a lieutenant-governor was found necessary the people permitted fees and licenses to be used for paying his salary, but it had been a free gift—nothing which they had been obliged to pay. They denied all desire to usurp power. They claimed, they said, only the right to dispose of their own money—a right guaranteed in their charter, the *natural right* of freeborn Englishmen, a right never before denied. They pointed out that it was impossible for an annually elected body to usurp power for any special class. They accused the governor of not wishing a reasonable bill.[70] He wanted, in their opinion, to kill the bill and throw the blame on the assembly, and he was glad of an opportunity to "make a fine speech" and, by showing his zeal, to secure a better position. What the governor and proprietor asked, they said, was *worse* than vassalage; vassals fight for their lord while he pays the bills "but our Lord would have us defend his Estate at our own Expense," which is "even more slavish than Slavery itself." The proprietor, they continued, asks them to "encrease and secure his Estate at our own Cost, and give him the glorious Privilege that no British Nobleman enjoys, of having his Lands free from Taxes, and defended gratis.'"[71] This presentation of their side of the case was about as strong as it could be made.

---

[70] Morris questioned the sincerity of the assembly as much as they did his. In a letter to DeLancey he said they did not wish to furnish assistance "and purposely started these disputes to furnish a pretence for their conduct. Had this been before a doubt, their last long message and refusal to establish a Militia would have made it clear." *Pa. Arch., 1748-56*, ii, 369.

[71] *Pa. Col. Rec.*, vi, 510, 525, 526 et seq., 569-585. They told Morris that several inhabitants of Philadelphia had offered to pay the proprietors' share of the £50,000 and rely on him to repay them. This they asserted was another proof of the justice of the tax, and they now hoped that the governor would sign the bill.

It was clear and concise although considerably overdrawn in some respects. A man less given to argument than Morris might have been overwhelmed by such an array of historical and legal data, but he was unconvinced and adhered to his demand for amendments.[72] Refusing to accept his amendments or to pass a militia act the assembly adjourned for a month, leaving the province without funds.

When they met again in September the controversy was renewed. After blaming the assembly for Braddock's defeat, the governor answered in detail the charges made by them during the preceding session. In reply to their statement that they did not enjoy "disputations" his answer was "But let your Minutes be examined for Fifteen years past, not to go higher, and in them will be found more artifice, more time and money spent in frivolous controversies, more unparalleled abuses of your Governors, and more undutifulness to the Crown, than in all the rest of his Majesty's colonies put together.''[73] The governor's statement was in the main true, but the inference which he wished to have drawn from it—that the assembly was entirely in the wrong—by no means followed. The proprietors whom he defended were still more selfish and equally as unyielding as the assembly. Excessive stubbornness on either side was responsible for the defenseless condition of the province.[74]

While the quarrel was in progress Morris appealed for aid to both Governor Belcher of New Jersey and General Shirley of Massachusetts, now commander of the king's forces, but both were unable and unwilling to assist a people who refused to defend themselves.[75]

---

[72] *Pa. Col. Rec.*, vi, 588.

[73] *Ibid.*, 623.

[74] Whether the proprietors should be taxed or not the governor would no longer dispute, declaring that it was sufficient for him "that they had given him no power in that case." "Those who would give up essential liberty to purchase a little temporary safety," answered the assembly, "deserve neither liberty nor safety." *Historical Review*, in Franklin, *Works*, iii, 422, 429.

[75] *Pa. Arch., 1748-56*, ii, 469, 471, 493 et seq., 502. Shirley a few days later authorized Morris to procure some ammunition and supplies from the king's stores at Cumberland, with the expectation that they would be replaced by the assembly.

Later in the session a compromise was arranged whereby money could be voted while either side maintained practically its original ground. After the news of Braddock's defeat had reached England the Penns, "intimidated," to quote Franklin, by the clamor raised against them "for their meanness and injustice in giving their governor such instructions," agreed to contribute £5000 as a free gift to be used for defense.[76] On receiving this news the assembly voted £55,000[77] in bills of credit without taxing the proprietary estates, "in consideration of their (proprietors) granting Five thousand pounds in lieu thereof." They made these bills payable within four years, thereby conforming to proprietary instructions, but without expressly conceding the point. The money was to be spent by a committee named in the act, but, for the first time, with the governor's approbation. Both sides were influenced apparently by the defeat of Braddock and by the new invasions of their province by the French who had won over tribes of Indians formerly friends of the English.[78]

For the same reasons the assembly at last consented to enact a militia law, which is an interesting example of Quaker political doctrines. Having set forth their conscientious scruples against bearing arms and the guarantees in their charter of privileges against being compelled to do so, they declared that "as the World is now Circumstanc'd" they did not wish to condemn the use of arms by others. The act was drawn by Franklin and simply gave legal sanction to the organization of companies from among those who should desire to enlist.[79] Such a law was little better than none at all, and Morris aptly pronounced it "senseless and impracticable." He believed, he said, that they had framed the bill thus for the purpose of compelling him to veto it, so he disappointed them by signing it.[80]

---

[76] *Works,* i, 196.

[77] Morris said £60,000 in a letter to Dinwiddie, Nov. 29.

[78] *Pa. Arch., 1748-56,* ii, 513-531. Various letters of Morris.

[79] *Ibid.,* 516. The act itself.

[80] "They have indeed passed a Militia Bill, but with no other view but that I should refuse it and then to raise a clamour against me on that acc't,

The above mentioned adjustment proved but a temporary lull in the controversy. It was renewed during the summer of 1756 and continued to the end of Morris's administration. Pleading his instructions, Morris refused to sign a bill for levying an excise on rum and other articles. His main objection was that the act did not give him any voice in spending the money to be raised. The assembly sent him resolutions to the effect that his instructions were "an infringement of their (our) Just rights," and that similar laws had been approved by the king, but no settlement could be reached.[81]

Soon after this the new governor, Denny, arrived, bringing with him a medal awarded to Franklin by the Royal Society. He made an effort to win the friendship of Franklin who was leader of the assembly, promising, the latter says, "adequate acknowledgements and recompenses" if the assembly could be induced to drop their opposition. Franklin assured the governor that his circumstances "were such as to make proprietary favors unnecessary" to him, and adds that "the disputes were renewed, and I was as active as ever in the opposition."[82]

The first meeting of the new governor with the assembly opened with more harmony than usual. One of the grievances thus far had been that former governors had refused to show their instructions to the assembly. That body had often expressed doubts that governors were bound by instructions to the extent which they pretended to be. Morris, especially, had been charged with exaggerating his instructions. When the assembly asked to see Denny's instructions on money bills, he complied at once with their request. They were now convinced that there had been no misrepresentation. They assured the governor that if these instructions were followed there could be no supplies voted, and asked if he could not sign a reasonable bill—such as the king had formerly approved—in spite of pro-

but as it is of such a nature as cannot be carried into execution, I have disappointed them, and given my consent to it." Morris to Sharpe, Nov. 26, 1755. *Ibid.*, 520.

[81] *Pa. Col. Rec.*, vii, 181, 185.
[82] *Works*, i, 214, 215.

prietary instructions.   Although they were informed by Denny
that he must conform to his instructions,[83] his yielding to their
request seems to have made a good impression on the assembly.
They passed an act for striking £30,000 in bills of credit to be
paid by an excise on rum and other spirits, and unlike the
similar bill presented to Morris, it was now provided that the
governor should have a voice in spending the money.[84]

This harmony was short-lived.   Verbal cannonading was
renewed in December (1756) over the quartering of British
soldiers.   Lord Loudoun had demanded winter quarters for his
troops and the governor asked the assembly to furnish them.
After some delay they passed a bill extending to Pennsylvania
the British act for quartering soldiers in public houses.   They
knew of course that there was not a sufficient number of public
houses to accommodate the army, but alleging that they had done
all that had been asked or could be expected of them, they
refused to do more.   So intent were they on proving their contention against the governor that they gave no thought to the
comfort of the troops and even refused sick soldiers the use of
their new provincial hospital.   When at last the governor
ordered the sheriffs to find quarters in private houses if necessary, the assembly yielded and provided the necessary quarters.[85]

The loss of this battle apparently made the assembly all the
more determined to win the next.   Once more did the proprietary estates become the paramount issue.   In January, 1757,
the assembly voted £100,000 for the king's service to be paid by
a tax on all estates, including those of the proprietors.   On the
refusal of Denny to sign the bill the assembly sent him a vigorous remonstrance demanding that the governor should sign it.
The bill, they said, violated neither charter, laws, nor royal

---

[83] *Pa. Col. Rec.*, vii, 237-239.

[84] *Ibid.*, viii, 40.   "I am glad," said Dinwiddie in a letter to Denny,
Nov. 12, "your Assembly voted £30,000 to be dispos'd of by your approbation, which has long been a Bone of Content^a."   *Pa. Arch., 1756-60*, iii, 50.

[85] *Pa. Col Rec.*, vii, 111-112, 364 et seq., 380.   "For the first Time since
the Charter," wrote the governor, "they sat all Saturday Afternoon and
Sunday Morning, and drew up a long abusive Message" on this subject.
To the proprietors, April 9, 1757.

instructions. Proprietary instructions, they maintained, were not laws, nor had they any binding force; for the proprietors had no right to obstruct grants to the king. Neither side would yield, and a similar bill failed for the same reason a month later.[86] It may be noted that here again they confuse the veto with *law-making*.

In persistency the governor was quite a match for the assembly, but not so in ingenuity. Taking advantage of the fact that a former and similar bill of theirs had been approved in England because of extreme need, they now made the present grant of £100,000 a supplement to the former act. But the Penns in the meantime had, with the approval of the Board of Trade, issued new orders forbidding the governor's assent to an act like that which the assembly had just supplemented. The assembly refused to make any alterations, and during the discussion which followed they stated their "rights" in no uncertain terms. By the terms of the supplementary bill all money not specifically appropriated was put at the disposal of the assembly. Because it was a money bill they demanded that it must be passed without amendment or alteration,[87] if not, the forces must be disbanded. They denied the governor's authority to prorogue or dissolve them, and claimed the right to adjourn themselves whenever and for so long a time as they pleased, without the governor's consent; and they insisted upon naming disbursing officers in their money bills. "In short," wrote Richards Peters of the council, "the Powers of Government are almost all taken out of the Hands of the Governor, and lodged in the Assembly; and as to what little remains, scarce a Bill comes up without an Attempt to lessen them."[88] As the Penns

---

[86] *Pa. Col. Rec.,* vii, 395-397, 409, 401-403.

[87] In a letter to the proprietors, April 9, Denny said that when he asked for a new bill, "Instead of Compliance, they thought proper to return to me the Bill with a Remonstrance, demanding it of me as their Right, 'to give my assent to it (and as it was a Money Bill without Alteration or Amendment) as I should answer to the Crown for all the Consequences of any Refusal at my peril.' " *Pa. Arch., 1756-60,* iii, 113.

[88] *Pa. Arch., 1756-60,* iii, 157. Penn wrote to Peters that he had "often been told by the greatest persons that there is no Government in Pennsylvania."

insisted that the governor should not allow "one Shilling" to be paid out without their consent and for purposes approved by them,[89] he was placed in a very difficult position. The charter of privileges gave the assembly, as they claimed, the right to "sit upon their own Adjournments," but if a strict construction of documents was to govern in all cases it would have to be admitted that both the royal charter and the charter of privileges gave the proprietors a coördinate power with them in the making of laws. This they were quite willing to overlook in their argument against proprietary instructions.

Loudoun now wrote to Denny that six months' pay was due the soldiers and that many were disbanding. Others refused to march until paid. He urged either side to yield some points for the present. The assembly made some minor alterations without conceding the main points at issue. Denny at last felt obliged to give way. In a verbal message he informed the assembly that he would sign their bill despite his instructions rather than involve the province in ruin.[90]

Having forced the governor to yield on this bill the assembly passed another more to his satisfaction (March 29, 1757). Military duty was made compulsory for all those not having scruples against bearing arms, except papists who must pay money instead. Control of the troops was put in the hands of the governor.[91]

Controversies in Pennsylvania were not confined to the larger problems of government. Insignificant points sometimes led to extended constitutional discussions in which the governors were quite as sensitive on questions of prerogative as the assemblies were jealous of their "rights." When Governor Denny was negotiating a treaty with the Delaware Indians in the spring of 1757, the Quakers wished to give an additonal string of wampum to the Indians, and asked the governor to send it with those given by the government. This offer he indignantly declined,

[89] *Pa. Arch., 1756-60,* iii, 157.

[90] *Ibid.,* 99; *Col. Rec.,* vii, 441, 453, 454, 448-449.

[91] *Pa. Arch, 1756-60,* iii, 120 et seq.

denouncing it as an attempt to infringe upon the prerogative of the king, who, through his agents, had the sole right to make treaties. The refusal was answered by a wordy defense of the Quakers by Joseph Galloway, the future loyalist, and by a remonstrance from the commissioners. In these documents it was asserted that most of the discontent on the part of the Indians had been caused by bad faith on the part of the Penns, and that the attempt of the Quakers to regain the good will of the Indians was both constitutional and laudable.[92] Exaggerated assertions were made[93] that the Quakers were inciting the Indians to make unreasonable claims, but the only foundation for this seems to have been the frequently expressed opinion of Quaker members that all disputes with the Indians might be peaceably settled by giving them their rights. The "religious prepossessions" of the Quakers, as Franklin said,[94] were "unchangeable" and "their obstinacy invincible," but there is no evidence of secret machinations on their part.

If the governor guarded jealously the treaty-making power of the king, the members of the assembly were equally alert in defending their "rights" against executive encroachments. At one of the regular conferences of governors called by the British commander in the summer of 1757, Governor Denny had agreed with Lord Loudoun and the southern governors to send two hundred troops from Pennsylvania to assist South Carolina. But they had not reckoned with the assembly, which body in a message (June 17) forcibly denied the governor's right to send troops out of the colony until a law for that purpose had been passed by the assembly.[95] As other assemblies interposed similar objections, executive and military officers were justified in thinking it unreasonable that valuable time must be lost in waiting the

---

[92] *Pa. Col. Rec.,* vii, 109, 656, 661; *Pa. Arch., 1756-60,* iii, 214-215.

[93] E. g., *ibid.,* 319.

[94] *Works,* iii, 16.

[95] *Pa. Col. Rec.,* vii, 575. Replying at the same time to a request for money for frontier defense, they informed the governor that money and laws had been supplied in plenty; if the frontiersmen suffered, it was due to the governor's own poor management. 577.

pleasure of several indifferent—often hostile— legislative bodies. Custom and in some cases the charter gave the assemblies the right to decide upon sending troops outside of their respective provinces, but they often carried this privilege to extremes and it was but natural that as soon as peace had been established the British government should turn its attention to a general readjustment of colonial control.

The old militia law had expired and an attempt to renew it in the summer of 1757 added another item to the controversy. Three bills which were sent to the governor were vetoed in succession on the ground that they were not "equitable and constitutional," but the main objection was that any one who wished to avoid military duty might plead a Quaker conscience and remain at home. All suggested amendments for the purpose of remedying this defect were termed religious tests worthy only of the days of the Inquisition,[96] but the assembly did not attempt to explain how officers were to distinguish Quakers from others without some kind of examination. They withheld from the governor the privilege of appointing officers except from a list of persons nominated by themselves,[97] but even this was more liberal than their former practice of naming officers in their bills.

A charge made by the assembly that the governor was partial to the lower counties (Delaware) brought a scathing denunciation of their conduct from the assembly of those counties. Our independence of the province of Pennsylvania, they said, we "esteem no small part of our Happiness." They resented any dictation from the province concerning the amount of money to be raised in the counties for defense. Usually the assembly of these counties maintained friendly relations with the governor, but in 1759 they adopted the tactics of their neighbors whom they

---

[96] "What the Governor means by an equitable and constitutional Militia Law we readily perceive by his amendments; a Law that will oblige the Inhabitants to take a Test as to their religious and Conscientious Scruples; if this be equitable and constitutional, it is the Equity and Constitution of Portugal or some other Popish countries where the inquisition is in use, and not any free Government, where the People enjoy their religious Liberties." *Pa. Col. Rec.,* vii, 744.

[97] *Pa. Col. Rec.,* vii, 744-745.

had criticized and forced him to sign bills which gave them full control of disbursements.[98]

In the spring of 1758 a controversy arose which continued during the rest of the war. The points at issue included the taxing of proprietary estates, the right of appointment to office, and the control of money voted for defense. At first the assembly's professions of loyalty to the king were profuse and their grants of money liberal. But knowing as that body did that the governor had been forbidden to sign such bills as they now offered him, it seems evident that their main purpose was to break the power of the proprietors either by forcing them to accept the terms of the assembly or by showing the British government that the Penns alone prevented the colony's loyal support of the crown. This they failed to accomplish, but the controversy is of interest because of the rather full discussion of many phases of constitutional authority.

In March, 1758, the assembly "earnestly solicitous that this Province may be distinguished among the Colonies for Loyalty, Ardour, and Zeal in defense of America," passed an act raising 2700 men to be united with troops from Virginia and Maryland under the command of General Abercrombie. They recommended a bounty of £5 for each volunteer. They granted to the king £100,000 in bills of credit to be paid by a tax on real and personal property—including the proprietary estates. The bill named as commissioners to spend this money some of their own members who had quarreled with the governor. The governor's approval of disbursements was not required. Governor Denny of course opposed the bill but offered to sign a separate bill for taxing proprietary estates, provided the owners were given some voice in the choice of assessors. As the people chose assessors to fix the tax on their property he urged that the Penns were entitled to a similar privilege. The assembly for a time refused to make any alterations, but they freely gave the governor their views on the constitutional points involved. His demand, they

---

[98] *Pa. Arch.*, *1756-60*, iii, 630, 634.

said, was "inconsistent with the Rights of the people" and only a scheme to exempt the proprietors from their proper share of the expenses. The House of Lords had never claimed the right to appoint commissioners to deal with financial matters; this was left wholly to the Commons. Money voted was a "free gift of the People of this Province to the Crown," and they denied the governor's right to obstruct such gifts, for the purpose of benefiting the proprietors. It is doubtless true that the offer was not made in good faith, but as the assembly would not discriminate between productive and unproductive estates, there was some justice in what the governor asked. The assembly agreed at last to exempt the estates altogether in the present bill—without conceding the right to impose such a tax—but they insisted that the money must be controlled by the commissioners appointed by the assembly from their own members. To give the governor the privilege of rejecting members selected to serve on the commission as he suggested was, in their opinion, equivalent to appointing them, for he could reject members until he had a majority in his favor.[99] Denny signed the bill in this form, but under protest.

The assembly replied to the governor's protest by denouncing severely both himself and the proprietors. The latter, they said, claimed greater powers and exemptions than either peers or royalty in England; the former had "usurped an arbitrary Power of amending Money Bills, and thereby repeatedly violated one of the most essential Rights of the People." He had prevented them from giving assistance to the crown. He had made no use of the men and money already voted, but had allowed the inhabitants to be butchered and permitted the enemies to go unpunished. They accused the governor and proprietors of being alone responsible for the weak condition of the colony.[100]

Whatever truth there may have been in these charges, their

[99] *Pa. Col. Rec.*, viii, 53, 63, 64, 67-69, 82, 83.

[100] *Ibid.*, 102-110. They told Denny that he had a greater eagerness for "fingering" the public money than they, and besides he is only a "Passenger, and regards not whether the Barque entrusted to his Care shall sink or Swim, provided he can by any means reach the shore."

own acts were not conducive to effective military operations. Holding rigidly to a "strict construction" policy in interpreting orders from the home government, they refused to supply General Forbes with tents, arms, and other camp necessaries on the ground that "the whole that the King expected or required from them (us), was the levying, cloathing and paying of the men." This they would do, but nothing more.[1] In December they again refused to vote aid to Forbes because it was a bad time of year. Nothing had been accomplished, they said, with the money previously voted, and besides they would be expected to contribute to the general fund, therefore, they would do nothing at present.[2] It matters little which party was most to blame in these contentions. It is of greater significance that either assembly or proprietor possessed, under such a system of government, the power to impede military operations and make imperial government both impotent and farcical.

In the fall of 1758 Franklin, who was then the assembly's agent in London, presented to the British officials a document called "Heads of Complaints." Its general purpose was to show that the Penns, by their arbitrary instructions to the governor, were preventing Pennsylvania from contributing toward the defense of the king's domains. These complaints were answered by F. J. Paris, agent for the Penns, who contended that only unreasonable bills had been vetoed. But the Penns evidently feared that the complaints might have some effect upon the attitude of the government, for they now declared their willingness to contribute whatever amount was found to be their proper proportion. It was their opinion, however, that they had already contributed more than their share.[3] Before the Privy Council gave an opinion on this matter other disputes had arisen.

In December Pitt again asked aid from Pennsylvania and the southern colonies, and assured them that the king would recommend reimbursement by Parliament. The Pennsylvania assembly

---

[1] *Pa. Col. Rec.*, viii, 112. Assembly to Governor Denny, May 3, 1758.

[2] *Ibid.*, 229.

[3] *Ibid.*, 279-281.

considered the matter until March (1759) and then replied that nothing would be granted until their grievances had been redressed. These grievances were illegal quartering of soldiers and taking of wagons by the troops without settling for them.

After the death of General Forbes the assembly refused to vote supplies until his successor should be ascertained. They had heard, they said, that the command was to be given to Colonel Byrd of Virginia, and if that were true, it would be useless to vote supplies, for no one would serve under him.[4] General Stanwix was appointed to the command, and whether his appointment satisfied the assembly or not, they and the people refused to give him any assistance. Stanwix informed Governor Denny that the people would not sell him conveyances for ready cash. The assembly was urged to authorize the impressment of conveyances, but that body simply replied that had the late General Forbes paid for what he had taken the people would now readily respond. Further legislation would be of no avail, for Stanwix himself paid little attention to laws or the people's rights.[5] Repeated appeals led only to repeated refusals.

The last controversy during Denny's administration resulted in a victory for the assembly. In June of 1759 they passed a bill granting a loan of £50,000 to Colonel Hunter of the king's army and authorizing the reissue of old bills. It also made quit-rents payable in currency. The last item was opposed by Richard Peters, secretary for the Penns and member of the council, who contended that this was a breach of contract. Both governor and council opposed the bill because it covered several distinct subjects, but the assembly would not alter it. The governor told the council that as he must accept this bill or nothing he intended to sign it. The council advised him not to yield, but Denny after accusing that body of having more solicitude for the interests of the proprietors than those of the king, signed the bill regardless of instructions.[6] This independent action of the governor was

---

[4] *Pa. Col. Rec.*, viii, 282, 297.

[5] *Ibid.*, 298, 344, 373-374.

[6] *Ibid.*, 342, 343, 350, 357, 358, 360.

probably due to the fact that he was soon to retire from office. It is evident also that he had become tired of the thankless task of defending the Penns in the extreme position which they had taken.

In July, 1759, Denny was succeeded by Hamilton who had been governor at the beginning of the war. According to a statement of Governor Sharpe of Maryland, Hamilton made it a condition of his acceptance that the proprietors permit him to use his own judgment in the matter of signing bills.[7] He found it necessary to make use of this privilege. No serious differences arose until the following March, when the assembly voted $100,000 in bills of credit, part of which was to be paid by a tax on proprietary estates. Hamilton seemed sincerely to desire a reasonable settlement of the tax question. He proposed several amendments which seem fair enough to both of the contending parties. He no longer asked that the proprietary estates be exempt from taxation, but that they should be rated no higher than other lands. He asked also that commissioners be appointed in each county to whom the proprietary agents might appeal if they considered the tax levied by the assessors unjust. Evidence submitted to the governor by Penn's secretary and receiver-general seems to show clearly that the assessors had either carelessly or purposely discriminated against the proprietors. Besides the changes just mentioned and a few other minor alterations Hamilton asked that disbursements be made with his approbation.

The assembly declined to accept any of the proposed amendments, and although Hamilton thought that the bill had been so framed for the purpose of compelling his veto and discrediting the proprietors in England, he signed it rather than hamper military operations by losing the money.[8]

[7] To William Sharpe, July 8, 1760, *Corresp. of Gov. Sharpe*, ii, 439. Sharpe thought that the Penns "richly deserved" criticism, for they made it impossible for any governor to deal harmoniously with the people. "The Proprietaries & their Govern[t] are become odious to the People & I believe some of the Dirt which has been thrown on them during the Contention will stick as long as their Names are had in remembrance."

[8] *Pa. Col. Rec.*, viii, 460-482; *Pa. Arch., 1756-60*, iii, 715.

So far the British government had taken no direct part in deciding the main questions at issue, but in June of 1760 a committee of the Privy Council took under consideration a bill which had been passed in Pennsylvania for reëmitting old bills of credit and taxing proprietary estates. This committee held that it was unfair to tax any proprietary estates which did not produce an income, or to tax any of them without giving the proprietors some voice in the selection of assessors. It was equally unfair, in their opinion, for the assembly to claim the exclusive right to spend the money voted. As to the appointment of officers created by their acts, the committee held that this was more than the House of Commons had ever claimed, for appointment is an executive power. It was also unjust, they said, to pay the proprietors in depreciated currency when sterling was caller for in the contracts; and the bills of credit were issued for too long a term. The committee's recommendation was that the king should veto the reëmitting acts, and the law taxing proprietary estates also unless it should be modified. The modifications required were to tax the estates the same as other lands, and to allow the governor the approval of all disbursements of money. The agents of the assembly, Franklin and Charles, agreed to these changes, but when the matter came before the assembly they flatly refused to carry out the agreement, giving as excuse that they had violated no law.[9]

From the reception of the king's veto until the end of the war the assembly did practically nothing to assist in military operations. They either refused to take any action whatever or else defied the royal veto by including in their bills measures which had been disapproved in England. Hamilton was of course bound by the decisions of the Privy Council and unable to sign bills which violated them.

In September, 1760, the governor urged the assembly to pass a bill for reënlisting troops to defend posts on Lake Erie and the Ohio, but after considering the matter for three days they

---

[9] *Pa. Col. Rec.,* viii, 524-557, 584; ix, 20.

decided to leave it to the next assembly.[10] They refused to respond to Pitt's call for troops in December because the king had annulled one of their laws and required amendment to another. It would be sacrificing their rights, they said, to pass laws of the kind desired.[11] In April, 1761, they voted £30,000, but included in the bill those points which had already been vetoed by the king. Hamilton tried to induce them to conform to the veto, but they would make no alterations.[12] In March, 1762, they granted £70,000 on the same old conditions and again the governor was obliged to veto. The assembly flatly refused to consider any amendments proposed and the matter had to be dropped.[13]

Nothing further was asked of the colony for hostilities were soon over. The king, however, was greatly incensed because of the perverse conduct of the assembly. After the preliminary peace was made with France and Spain, the Earl of Egremont sent a letter to Hamilton (November 27, 1762) in which he stated that although the war had ended and further aid would be unnecessary, the king wished to express his displeasure with the assembly for their disregard of his veto. Their manner of framing bills on impossible terms, he said, was considered equivalent to refusing aid altogether.[14]

MARYLAND

In Maryland the conditions were much like those in Pennsylvania. Here as in the latter colony three parties figured in the controversy—the assembly which represented the people, the proprietor with his own special interests, and the home government which considered only the interests of the empire as a whole. Not only were the conditions similar to those in Pennsylvania but the assembly of Maryland watched closely the acts

---

[10] *Pa. Col. Rec.,* viii, 495-496.
[11] *Ibid.,* 588, 596 et seq.
[12] *Ibid.,* 605 et seq.
[13] *Ibid.,* 693 et seq.
[14] *Ibid.,* ix, 15, 16.

of the Pennsylvania assembly and adopted its ideas and measures of resistance to executive authority.

The governor, whose duty it was to secure legislation satisfactory to each of the opposing parties, had a very difficult task to perform. The king's secretary of state would send orders to the governor for men and money. The governor's power to approve laws was limited by proprietary instructions. The assembly in turn demanded the passage of laws which were contrary to those instructions, otherwise they would not vote the assistance desired by the king. As in Pennsylvania, both proprietor and assembly preferred as a rule to let the colony go defenseless rather than yield in matters under discussion. While the desire to overthrow proprietary government is not so patent here as in Pennsylvania, it appears at times, and there is little doubt that bills were often presented to the governor with the hope that their expected veto would discredit the proprietor in England. An old law passed in 1649 and approved by Cecil Calvert gave the assembly a means of hampering general military operations whenever they saw fit to use it. By this law the proprietor and his heirs could not, without the consent of the assembly, require the freemen "to Aid or Assist with their Persons or Estates" in a war outside the colony.[15]

When Governor Dinwiddie of Virginia was planning the Ohio expediton in the spring of 1754 the Maryland assembly at first refused to vote assistance. They granted £3000 to be used at the Albany convention for presents to the Indians, but as the amount was to be taken from the income from fines and licenses claimed by the proprietor, the bill was vetoed by the governor. Later in the summer after Washington's defeat the assembly voted £6000 toward assisting the Virginians against the French, but as they would vote nothing to pay for conveyances, the people refused to furnish them. Both horses and wagons had to be pressed into service. This fell unequally on the inhabitants and caused much bitterness.[16]

---

[15] *Corresp. of Gov. Sharpe,* ii, 475.
[16] *Ibid.,* i, 56, 68, 71, 88, 211.

Governor Sharpe of Maryland was appointed commander-in-chief of the forces in the southern colonies and at the end of the year 1754 he had but a single company which had been raised in his own province.[17]   Sharpe wrote to Sir Thomas Robinson (January 12, 1755) that his assembly would vote nothing because of the example and influence of Pennsylvania.   About a month later they voted £10,000 for the king's service, but as it was to be taken from the income from fines and licenses, the bill was rejected by the council, who claimed that by the charter this belonged to the proprietor.[18]   This income from fines and licenses was the chief bone of contention in Maryland—the obstacle which most frequently delayed or prevented the passage of money bills.   It was a disputed question whether this income rightfully belonged to the government of the colony or to the proprietor.   The governor himself had no certain knowledge on this point.   In the summer of 1755, while he was contemplating the veto of a bill just passed by the assembly granting £5000, he wrote to his brother John[19] asking the latter's authority for deciding that this money belonged to the proprietor.   In his letter Sharpe gave a history of the disposal of this money in the past which seems to show that the assembly was right in its claim that this income belonged to the colony.   Originally, he said, the income from fines and licenses belonged to the proprietor, but had been taken from him by William III.   On several occasions it had been restored to the Baltimores by temporary laws, but at other times it had been appropriated by the government of the colony.   The last law on the subject was passed in 1746 when the government had appropriated this money for an intended expedition against Canada.   This law was still (1755) in force.[20]   But the bill just enacted by the assembly never reached the governor, for the council rejected it

---

[17] *Pa. Arch., 1748-56*, ii, 215.   Shirley to Morris, Dec. 17, 1754.

[18] *Corresp. of Gov. Sharpe*, i, 165, 172, 360-362.

[19] John Sharpe was a member of Parliament.   His advice was sought frequently by Secretary Calvert.

[20] *Corresp. of Gov. Sharpe*, i, 235.

on account of the provision concerning licenses. Being unable to agree on a law members from both houses and other individuals subscribed money, just before Braddock's defeat, to support a company of volunteer rangers.[21] Members of the assembly declared that nothing would ever induce them to give up the income from fines and licenses, and those of the council were equally unyielding. Had Baltimore been as determined as the Penns to sacrifice the public good for his own private interests no bills could have passed, but after Braddock's defeat he gave up all claim to both fines and licenses, and by special instructions ordered the governor to sign bills in which they were appropriated to the common cause.[22]

Military duty afforded another element of discord. When the war broke out there was no adequate militia law in Maryland and the assembly persistently refused to enact one. Without such a law the governor was unable to carry out the orders of the British secretary of state or those of the British generals in America. Unless in very urgent cases, the inhabitants could hardly be expected to neglect their business affairs and leave their families exposed to attack, without some guarantee of compensation. The few who did enlist were sadly neglected. Sharpe estimated that the militia numbered from 16,000 to 20,000 men, but there was no law which compelled them to serve in the army or authorized discipline for those who did enlist.[23] One-third of the number were without arms of any kind and the remainder had very poor ones. The officers who recruited troops for the British regiments had to resort principally to indentured servants,[24] but this led to opposition and riots on the part of the planters. None of these conditions would the assembly even attempt to remedy. Sharpe attributed their attitude largely to the influence of Pennsylvania, but it is evident that they needed

---

[21] *Corresp. of Gov. Sharpe,* i, 363, 368. Copy of report to Board of Trade.
[22] *Ibid.,* i, 368.
[23] *Ibid.,* 353. Civil officers, tradesmen, convicts, and Catholics were exempt from military duty.
[24] *Ibid.,* 211.

little tutoring when it was a question of opposing authority.[25] One of the leading members suggested that the people be recommended to provide themselves with arms and to learn to use them, "but that every Step farther than that would abridge the Liberty to which as Englishmen they have an inviolable Right."[26] If this were a true interpretation of English rights, Great Britain would soon lose her place among the powerful nations of the world.

Even if their "rights as Englishmen" could not be harmonized with a compulsory militia law, it is difficult to understand why those rights should prevent the assembly from accepting the assistance of several tribes of Indians who offered aid if the colony would supply them with provisions. But they were so "excessively parcimoneous" according to Sharpe, that they would allow provisions for none except those on the roll of the colony, which were very few. The governor was not permitted even to entertain Indians as guests at public expense, although much depended on their friendship.[27]

The laws already in force empowered the governor to compel every individual[28] of military age to march to any part of the province where his services were needed, but the assembly declared by resolution in 1758 that this applied only to cases of actual invasion by the enemy.[29] Such an interpretation of the law made any precautionary measures depend entirely on the will of the assembly, which was not always in session.

After Baltimore gave up his claim to the income from fines and licenses, the assembly framed their money bills in such a way that he would have to yield in still another matter or be placed in the undesirable position of obstructing grants to the king. Again influenced, as Sharpe thought, by Pennsylvania, they passed a bill in the spring of 1756 granting £40,000 for

---

[25] *Corresp. of Gov. Sharpe,* i, 219, 222, 257, 353; *Pa. Arch., 1748-56,* ii, 397.

[26] *Corresp. of Gov. Sharpe,* i, 491. Sharpe to Calvert, Oct. 5, 1756.

[27] *Ibid.,* 549. Sharpe to Dinwiddie, May 5, 1757.

[28] Except certain exempted classes.

[29] *Corresp. of Gov. Sharpe,* ii, 255.

the king's service. Of this amount £25,000 was to be used for an expedition against the enemy, but they took the precaution to provide that it could not be so used unless Virginia and Pennsylvania would assist. One of the means provided for raising this amount was a tax on lands, including those of Lord Baltimore. With respect to the land tax Baltimore was quite as selfish as the Penns and had ordered the governor not to pass any law which did not exempt his lands, but the assembly was determined that they should be taxed. By adopting a conservative course Sharpe avoided a prolonged controversy like that in Pennsylvania. He was not entirely in sympathy with the claims of the assembly and considered them "too opinionated" and "parsimoneous" to provide sufficient money for defense unless they could "subvert in a great measure the Constitution & render it more similar to that of Pennsilvania," but he did not, he told his brother, feel called upon to follow the example of Governor Morris and uphold unreasonable proprietary instructions at the expense of the welfare of the province. As the upper house also took this view of the matter the bill was passed in spite of instructions to the contrary.[30] Having settled this matter amicably the assembly a little later voted £3000 to be used in raising men for the Royal American regiment, and £2000 toward furnishing the New York army with transports and wheat. But they refused to send men to New York and likewise to grant Secretary Robinson's request for a compensation to masters whose servants had been enlisted by the recruiting officers.[31]

Besides being very economical in voting money for defense the assembly unreasonably demanded exclusive control of the movement of troops. Regardless of the fact that efficient military service requires executive control, and in spite of law and custom in their own colony, they insisted on dictating the time and place in which the troops should be used and under whom they should serve.

---

[30] *Corresp. of Gov. Sharpe*, i, 346, 391, 395, 399, 400, 403-404, 415, 424, 425, 435; *Pa. Arch., 1748-56*, ii, 685.

[31] *Corresp. of Gov. Sharpe*, i, 494.

When the Earl of Loudoun was sent to command the British forces in America the colonies as usual were asked to assist him. The Maryland assembly voted to contribute a small sum which was then in the treasury, but no more. They inserted a clause directing how and where Maryland troops must be employed. They were not to serve under Loudoun either within the province or outside its borders. Within the province Loudoun must not have even indirect control over the men. Colonel Stanwix, but no one else, might take the troops out of the colony. This conflicted with the plans of Loudoun who had ordered the Maryland troops to garrison Fort Cumberland, and it is difficult to see why he was not justified in pronouncing the act "inconsistent in itself, and a direct infringement of the King's undoubted prerogative . . . . of commanding all Troops in his Dominions"; but the governor decided to accept these terms rather than lose the appropriation. Governor Dinwiddie of Virginia commended Sharpe for accepting the grant even on these terms, but added that the "ill-natur'd Opposition" and "unmannerly" conduct of the lower house in Maryland had caused him much trouble with his own assembly.[32]

In the fall of 1757 when Loudoun again asked Maryland to furnish provisions for troops at Fort Cumberland the assembly declared by resolution that they would never vote a thing for them as long as they remained at that post.[33] They formally condemned the disposition which Loudoun had made of the troops during the preceding summer and announced that they were about to reduce the entire force of the colony to three hundred rangers who were to protect the frontier settlements. Before this they had taken into their own hands practically everything connected with the army. A committee appointed by the assembly had entire charge of feeding and clothing the men. The governor was given no voice in this or in the dis-

[32] *Corresp. of Gov. Sharpe*, ii, 3, 24.

[33] *Ibid.*, 91, 123, 126. A small number of Maryland troops had already been taken there, but it was a disputed point whether this fort was situated in Maryland. The lower house wanted to give up this post and the surrounding territory.

bursement of other public money.[34] Such acts were more than mere precautionary measures. Such a policy was an unreasonable and unnecessary impediment to any general campaign.

A law of the province provided that whenever the militia should be called out to defend the province the expense should be paid by a poll-tax. Instead of employing this customary tax to support the three hundred rangers, the assembly proposed a tax on real and personal property, offices, professions, proprietary quit-rents and ecclesiastical preferments. Assessors were to be appointed by special commissioners chosen by the people, and these commissioners were to have absolute control of the troops.[35] The governor and council would not approve the bill on these terms, and the former wrote Baltimore that nothing could be expected from the colonies until they were compelled by Parliament to furnish their respective quotas.[36] Again he attributed the conduct of the assembly and their influence over the people to the teachings of the *Pennsylvania Gazette*. From that source they had derived the doctrine that "the Upper House is no Part of our Constitution," and it "is from that Quarter that all our Fine Schemes are imported."[37]

In order to get around the law which gave the governor control of the militia the assembly resorted to an interesting example of strict construction. Sharpe had planned to garrison Fort Frederick with militia, but the assembly presented a remonstrance denying his authority to do so. The militia, they argued, were not obliged to march under the governor's orders except in cases of *actual* invasion. Besides, they could not be compelled to garrison forts or to serve in arms at all unless there were "an Apparent Enemy within the Limits of the Province." The ravages which had been committed on the frontiers were not "Invasions," but "only Incursions." They agreed to furnish Loudoun with two hundred men *provided he would not take*

---

[34] *Corresp. of Gov. Sharpe*, ii, 31, 51.

[35] *Ibid.*, 100-101.

[36] *Ibid.*, 111-112.

[37] *Ibid.*, 120. To Calvert, Dec. 27, 1757.

them out of Maryland, but they immediately reconsidered this generous offer and withdrew it.[38]

Soon after this the assembly granted £45,000 for military purposes but on terms which the council pronounced unconstitutional. A conference was arranged by the governor, but as the representatives of the lower house were instructed to concede nothing, the conference ended in failure and the assembly was prorogued without granting anything for defense. Nothing could be obtained without absolute submission to the will of the lower house, or, to quote Sharpe himself, there was no course left for the governor and council but to consider how they might "yield most decently to every demand that the Lower House of Assembly shall think proper to make."[39]

There is apparently much truth in Sharpe's claim that the attitude of the lower house was influenced in a large measure by a desire to discredit proprietary government in the eyes of the king.[40] But unlike the governors of Pennsylvania Sharpe did not throw the entire blame on the assembly. Toward the end of the war he wrote his brother that their obstinacy was due in great measure to the unreasonable claims of the proprietor. Baltimore for a time demanded the income from fines and licenses which did not belong to him, and because of this, said Sharpe, the assembly determined to strip him of as much power as possible. Both Sharpe and his brother considered it the duty of British generals—not of the assembly—to supply money for the commissary department.[41]

---

[38] *Corresp. of Gov. Sharpe,* ii, 141-142. Sharpe to Loudoun, March 2, 1758.

[39] *Ibid.,* 146, 181, 186.

[40] "The Truth is that their leading Men (. . . .) are anxious to bring every thing into Confusion in hopes that the Crown will then think it necessary to interfere in some manner or other that might be disagreeable to his Lordship." "Were they to refuse to grant any money for His Majesty's Service their Constituents would unanimously condemn their Conduct, but while they can save Appearances so far as to appear fond of granting Supplies the People will be imposed on & made to believe that the Upper House & the Governor are alone to blame, & it is entirely owing to the Government of Maryland & Pensa being in the hands of Proprietors that Money for His Majesty's Service is not so readily granted in these Provinces as in the other Colonies." Sharpe to Calvert, May 14, 1756, *ibid.,* ii, 179.

[41] *Ibid.,* ii, 439-441. Sharpe to William Sharpe, July 8, 1760.

In order to overcome opposition to the proprietor in the two houses of assembly Secretary Calvert[42] was ready to employ measures which were not unlike those of the modern political boss. His scheme was carefully to select members for the upper house, and to bribe those of the lower house with appointive offices. In a letter to Sharpe, March 17, 1760, Calvert outlined a plan to be followed by the governor. When choosing members of the upper house he advised the governor not to "admit a fool who will not only be troublesome & Impertinent but will Blabb every thing he knows." Neither should he appoint a man of ability who was not known to be favorable to the proprietor— for in that case, the more able the man the more dangerous he would be in the council.

Having provided for the council, Calvert proceeded to show Sharpe how the lower house might easily be made subservient. In nineteen out of twenty cases, he said, members oppose measures from private interest, "therefore by throwing out a Sop in a proper manner to these Noisy animals it will render them not only silent, but tame enough to bear stroking & tractable enough to follow any directions that may be thought fit to be given to them." This "Sop" he explained in detail, but in substance the plan was that members of the lower house were to be given to understand that if they did as Calvert desired while members, they need not fear the people, for all members who should fail to be reëlected because of loyalty to the proprietor would be rewarded with other offices. Among these were the offices of sheriff, farmer of the quit-rents, etc. If members did not wish these offices for themselves, their brothers or sons would receive the commissions. Calvert had calculated to a nicety just the number of members it would be necessary to "Bait" in this way.[43]

Whether Lord Baltimore was cognizant of this plan to cor-

---

[42] Cecil Calvert, uncle and secretary of the proprietor.

[43] There are 58 members, he said, but usually not all attend. "Now the business is to find Baits for 30 of these; which is a clear Majority, supposing they were all to attend." Calvert to Sharpe, March 17, 1760. *Corresp. of Gov. Sharpe*, ii, 376-379.

rupt the assembly does not appear in the records. It was never put to a test, for Calvert's suggestions were not followed. Sharpe opposed the elaborate scheme, not on moral grounds it would seem from his answer to Calvert, but because he considered the plan impracticable. Baltimore's friends, he said, usually get all such offices so that the governor has none to distribute; besides, members of the lower house as a rule are not qualified to fill such offices—many of them can scarcely write.[44] The last item of information is of interest when we consider that these same members felt themselves fully capable of deciding all points of constitutional law—better qualified, apparently, than the king's attorney-general.

Very little was contributed by Maryland during the last year and a half of the war. Five times within less than eighteen months did the lower house pass bills embodying points which the king's attorney-general had pronounced unlawful, and each time the upper house refused to concur. Neither would give way although the enemy was ravaging the frontier. Whenever the attention of the lower house was called to the opinion of the attorney-general their answer was simply that *they did not agree with him.*[45] His opinion seemed to impress them no more than that of the least able of their own members.

There was little apparent loyalty to the interests of the mother country[46] or respect for authority. On the other hand the proprietor cared only for his own interests. The end of the war relieved the pressure of opposing interests, but it was certain to reappear under similar conditions.

While proprietary government in itself was not entirely responsible for the discord in Maryland and Pennsylvania, no small part of it is traceable directly to this anomalous creation of British rulers. Attributes of sovereignty combined with ownership of the soil worked badly wherever it was tried. To obtain sufficient revenue for governmental purposes was difficult

[44] *Corresp. of Gov. Sharpe,* ii, 423-431. Sharpe to Calvert, July 7, 1760.
[45] *Ibid.,* 394, Sharpe to Pitt, April 14, 1760.
[46] *Ibid.,* 397. Sharpe to Baltimore, May 4, 1760.

enough in all of the colonies, but the introduction of another factor to separate still farther sovereign from subject added to the expense and confused legitimate requirements with proprietary greed, in the minds of the people.

IV. THE SOUTHERN COLONIES

VIRGINIA

When the French appeared on the Ohio, Virginia had a greater interest in preventing their encroachments than any other colony. She was interested in extending her claims westward and the presence of the French caused her much concern. As soon as the plans of the French were discovered Governor Dinwiddie took steps to drive out the invaders and hold the country for England. While the initiative devolved upon Virginia, the neighboring colonies were asked for assistance. It has already been noted that for some time Pennsylvania and Maryland would do absolutely nothing, and, as will appear further on, the southern colonies did very little.

Dinwiddie was forced to rely principally on his own colony for sinews of war, and unfortunately for the success of his plans, the conditions were not favorable even there. Without the coöperation of the assembly the governor was powerless, for that body controlled the finances of the colony; and the members at this time were in no mood to coöperate with a governor who was attempting, in their opinion, to deprive them of their "inherent" and "British rights." A controversy was already in progress when the enemy made his appearance, and little could be done in defense of the colony until constitutional questions had been settled.

In 1753 Governor Dinwiddie for the first time attempted to collect a fee of one pistole[47] for affixing the official seal to land patents. In November of that year inhabitants from several counties petitioned the house of burgesses for protection against this new burden.[48] The burgesses sent an address to Dinwiddie

---

[47] A Spanish coin worth about $3.50.

[48] *Journals of the House of Burgesses, 1752-1758,* 121, 129. All references to the *Journals* refer to this volume.

asking whether the fee demanded at the secretary's office had been charged by the governor's order, if so, by what authority.[49] Dinwiddie replied that he had ordered the fee collected and gave as his authority the advice of his council and "Powers from Home."[50] The first part of his statement was true, but the "Powers from Home" were largely imaginary. Not convinced by the proofs submitted by the governor, the house of burgesses sent him a vigorous protest declaring his action unlawful. They based their interference in the land question on the "undoubted Right of the Burgesses to enquire into the Grievances of the People," any abridgment of which would be dangerous to their liberties and to the constitution of the colony. "The Rights of the Subject," they asserted, "are so secured by Law, that they cannot be deprived of the least Part of their Property, but by their own Consent." Upon this excellent principle, they said, their constitution had been founded, and the king had declared " 'That no Man's Life, Member, Freehold of Goods, be taken away or harmed, but by established and known Laws.' "[51] It will be seen at once that the burgesses had constructed a huge man of straw for the purpose of demolishing him. The excellence of the principles invoked can not be gainsaid, but their relevancy is more than doubtful as Dinwiddie pointed out in his answer.[52] However unjust the imposition of the fee may have been it related solely to the disposal of the king's lands—the purchase of which was optional on the part of the buyer—and not to taxation or the administration of government.

More to the point was the other argument of the burgesses based on precedent and royal charter. The governor's attention was called to the fact that no such fee had been exacted by the old Virginia Company, and that Charles II by charter had ordained that the method of the old company should be continued. Lord Howard of Effingham had attempted, they said, to exact a fee

[49] *Journals*, 136.

[50] *Ibid.*, 141.

[51] *Ibid.*, 143-144; *Dinwiddie Papers*, i, 46.

[52] *Journals*, 154.

for the use of the seal, but had been forbidden to do so by William III and his Privy Council. Upon this representation the governor was requested to withdraw his order for collecting the fee.

When the governor declined to rescind his order to the secretary and declared that he was more than ever convinced of its justice, the burgesses were so incensed that they passed a series of resolutions condemning his action and providing for an appeal to the crown. The governor's action in demanding the fee they pronounced "illegal and arbitrary"—a violation of charter rights and a subversion of their constitution. It was a hinderance to settlement and therefore detrimental to both king and subject. They resolved to send Attorney-General Randolph to England as special agent to protest to the king against the conduct of the governor. Although they pleaded poverty when asked for money to defend the colonies, the burgesses agreed to pay Randolph £2,500 for his services, and promised him a pension in case he should lose his office of attorney-general on account of his mission. The king, however, was especially petitioned to continue Randolph in his office. When the council refused to allow this salary the house of burgesses on their own responsibility voted to deduct that amount from the crown revenues, and the treasurer was directed to pay it without the concurrence of either council or governor. The treasurer, who was also speaker of the house, expressed his willingness to carry out their order, but the governor would not issue a warrant for the money.[53]

Their appeal to the crown caused Dinwiddie considerable anxiety and he admitted to his agent in England that he never would have taken the fee had he known that so much trouble would come from it. He was particularly annoyed because it had made "so much Noise in the Coffee Houses" in England.[54] The Privy Council compromised the matter by rejecting the petition of the burgesses but forbidding the collection of a fee on tracts

---

[53] *Journals*, 154-156, 167-169; *Din. Pap.*, i, 72, 140, 160.

[54] *Din. Pap.*, i, 137-139. To James Abercromby, April 26, 1754.

under 100 acres. This was practically what the burgesses had
asked. Dinwiddie now threw the entire blame on the council and
declared that he, personally, had never desired to collect the
fee.[55] The payment of Randolph's salary still remained a bone
of contention and impeded the voting of supplies.

While the pistole question was pending in England the house
of burgesses voted £10,000 for frontier defense, although one of
their prominent members questioned the king's title to the Ohio
Valley.[56] With this first war bill the burgesses adopted a practice which they continued to follow although it was pronounced
unconstitutional by the governor. In the body of the bill they
named directors whose duty it was to decide how the money
should be spent. But they did not deprive the governor of his
right to approve appropriations as was done in Pennsylvania.
Their "republican Principles" Dinwiddie denounced in various
letters, and he declared that necessity alone induced him to sign
such a bill.[57] Anxiety over the pistole affair no doubt helped to
secure his signature, but aside from this he was too politic to
carry resistance to extremes. He frankly admitted that he had
no influence over his assembly[58] and a year later he expressed his
belief that crown instructions should be suspended when urgency
required it.[59] He thought the governor and assembly of Pennsylvania differed over trifles while the colonies were in danger, and
he believed that proprietary estates should be taxed the same as
other property.[60] Although Dinwiddie met with opposition at
times, he secured more money from a reluctant assembly than
any other governor south of New England.

Even after money had been voted by the assembly great difficulty was experienced in getting men to enlist except those of

---

[55] *Din Pap.*, i, 262, 263, 370. To the Board of Trade, Oct. 25, 1754.

[56] *Ibid.*, 102; Hening, *Statutes*, vi, 417 et seq.

[57] *Din Pap.*, i, 103, and other letters.

[58] "W't Influence You may have over Y'r Assembly I know not, but I
frankly tell You I have none over this here, further than arguing on the
necessity and leaving the Quantum to them." To Gov. Glen of S. C., April
15, 1754. *Din. Pap.*, i, 128.

[59] *Ibid.*, ii, 29.

[60] *Ibid.*, i, 507; ii, 181.

the poorest quality, and the militia law in force was extremely inadequate. Under the latest militia law, passed in 1748,[61] the militia could not be taken from the colony. The pay of the troops was small and they were obliged to equip themselves. Provisions and conveyances might be pressed into service but not until they had been appraised and proper allowance made to the owners, all of which consumed considerable time. Many of the soldiers feared that they would never receive even the small pay allowed by this law, and refused to serve. Washington frequently complained of the bad condition of those already in the ranks.[62] The officers, he said, were threatening to resign for lack of pay. He wished to serve without pay rather than accept such a small amount and be uncertain of getting that. He would rather "dig for a maintenance . . . . than serve upon such ignoble terms."[63] Little could be accomplished under such conditions, and it was some time before the governor and assembly could sufficiently harmonize their opinions on constitutional questions to provide for defense. Practically no assistance was received at first from other colonies, and Dinwiddie proposed to Lord Halifax and other British officials that a poll-tax be levied in all the colonies for war purposes.[64]

When the assembly met in August, 1754, Dinwiddie again asked them to vote money for defense. The burgesses commended Dinwiddie for his prudent measures in defeating the designs of the French, but at the same time they embraced this opportunity to force the governor to accept their terms. They voted £20,000 for the king's service but attached as a rider the payment of Randolph's salary of £2,500 for his services in Eng-

[61] Hening, vi, 112 et seq.

[62] Washington, *Writings* (Ford's ed.) i, 42. "We daily experience the great necessity for Cloathing the men, as we find the generality of those, who are to be enlisted, are of those loose, idle persons, that are quite destitute of house and home, and, I may truly say, many of them are cloathless; . . . . There are many of them without shoes, others want stockings, some are without shirts, and not a few that have scarce a coat or waistcoat to their backs." See also pp. 130 et seq.

[63] *Ibid.*, 63-65.

[64] *Din. Pap.*, i, 238, 251.

land—the same that Dinwiddie had previously refused to allow. The governor agreed to pass the rider as a separate bill provided they would insert a clause suspending its operation until the king's will should be ascertained, but the burgesses insisted on the passage of the bill as it stood.[65] Accusing them of hypocrisy and severely denouncing their conduct, Dinwiddie prorogued the assembly without procuring the necessary supplies. I "See you call'd upon," said he, "in ye Day of your Country's Distress; hear you declaring your knowledge of her Danger, and professing the most ardent Zeal for her Service; yet find these declarat'ns only an unavailing Flourish of Words . . . . You withhold Y'r aid and thereby leave the Enemy at full Liberty to perpetuate their destructive and unjust designs."[66] Before being prorogued the burgesses asked the governor to express their thanks to the king for his paternal care in sending his independent companies from New York and South Carolina to defend their colony; but excused themselves from granting supplies to these same companies and hoped that his Majesty would be "graciously pleased" to provision them himself.[67]

The assembly convened again in October and the governor in his address painted the impending perils in glowing colors, regretting that he could not find words to make it more soul-stirring. In an equally effusive reply the assembly promised their hearty support, assuring the governor that no harm would ever come to the colony through their neglect.[68] They passed two acts which they considered very magnanimous, but which were not conducive to successful military operations. Both conformed to old principles, and the militia act very largely counteracted the benefits derived from the other. The militia act[69] permitted the enlistment of "such able bodied men, as do not follow or exercise any lawful calling or employment, or have some other

[65] *Journals*, 198; *Din. Pap.*, i, 298-300, 328.
[66] *Journals*, 205; *Din. Pap.*, i, 302, 328; *Col. Rec. of N. C.*, v, 138.
[67] *Journals*, 200.
[68] *Ibid.*, 209, 211.
[69] Hening, *Statutes*, vi, 438-439.

lawful and sufficient support or maintenance," for that particular expedition. All who were entitled to vote for members of the house of burgesses were exempted from service. The act was to remain in force for one year. So jealously did the burgesses guard the "rights" of the people that only vagrants could be enlisted for duty outside of the province, and even they could not be forced to enlist. This house opposed all draft laws as violating their rights as Englishmen. Such was the kind of soldiers sent to defend the empire; it is little wonder that Washington continually complained of the personnel of his army.

By the other act the assembly granted £20,000 toward the expenses of the expedition. As usual the disbursement was put in the hands of directors, but all payments required the governor's approval. Dinwiddie accepted the grant on these terms more graciously than before and "parted with the (our) Assembly on very good Terms."[70]

Little assistance came from the surrounding colonies.[71] Neither their country's interests nor their own danger could overcome the indifference of the people or their representatives;[72] but they were keenly alive on questions relating to their rights and privileges. But the executives who criticised the assemblies were equally headstrong and unyielding. While the strife continued the inhabitants were being butchered and their property destroyed.

The arrival of Braddock caused nearly all of the colonies to vote some additional assistance. But the general's first experience with Virginia was not a happy one. On May 15, 1755, he sent a letter to Dinwiddie stating that he would remove all effective troops from Fort Cumberland and asking the governor

---

[70] *Din. Pap.*, i, 409. To James Abercromby, Nov. 16, 1754.

[71] Dinwiddie wrote on March 17, 1755, that the neighboring colonies had not granted "any Assist'ce either in Money, Men or Provis's, except N. York, ab't 3,000 St'g; No. Car., 6,000, their money; M'yl'd the same sum; So. Car. and Pensylv'a, not a Farthing." *Col. Rec. of N. C.*, v, 394-395.

[72] "but truly I think," wrote Dinwiddie to Halifax concerning all the colonies, "in gen'l, they have given their Senses a long Holliday." *Din. Pap.*, i, 513.

to garrison it with militia. The assembly at once protested that such a measure was contrary to law, as the fort was located in Maryland, and also that the expense would "tend to the utter Ruin of this Colony." Dinwiddie reminded them that Fort Cumberland had been built to protect the colonies in general and rightly said that "it is of no Consequence whether it is in *Virginia* or *Maryland;* it is the King's Fort, and the Guns mounted there, are those sent by his Majesty for such Uses." The burgesses yielded temporarily to the extent of introducing a bill to draft not more than fifty men for this purpose, but the bill was rejected at its third reading.[73] For the western expedition the burgesses granted £10,000 and agreed to raise two hundred men for frontier defense.[74]

The defeat of Braddock in July caused great consternation in Virginia, and for a time aroused some enthusiasm for the British cause. When the assembly met in August they readily voted another £40,000 and enacted a more effective militia law.[75] The last two amounts voted were in bills of credit instead of sterling, but payable within the five year limit fixed by the British government. As there was great need of money for war purposes the governor, although opposed to paper money, signed the bills without protest.

The militia bill just passed proved inadequate. At the October session the governor urged the passage of a law similar to the British militia act, but his recommendation was disregarded. Up to this time controversies over paper money, so frequent in some of the other colonies, had not appeared in Virginia, but during this session the house of burgesses seemed to have caught the contagion. They passed an act for issuing £200,000 in paper money to be current for eight years. This would impair the credit of the colony to a degree that the governor was not willing to permit and he refused to sign the bill. After several alterca-

---

[73] *Journals,* 267, 268, 272, 284.

[74] *Din. Pap.,* ii, 86.

[75] Honing, *Statutes,* vi, 521 et seq.; *Din. Pap.,* ii, 142; *Journals,* 314.

tions concerning the constitutionality of the bill, Dinwiddie dissolved the assembly and waited for a new election.[76]

At the beginning of 1756 little had been done to prevent the encroachments of the enemy. The money which had been raised could not be used effectively so long as the people refused to enter the service. Dinwiddie recommended to the Lords of Trade that convicts sentenced to transportation should be sent to serve at the frontier forts.[77] The militia according to the governor's estimate numbered about 3,600, but nearly all of them were freeholders who insisted on their privilege of not serving except in cases of imminent danger, and then only within the province. With the enemy at their door it took four months to enlist less than five hundred recruits, and these were of an inferior class.[78] Washington wrote from the frontier of the distress of the inhabitants, and saw nothing ahead but "inevitable destruction" unless the assembly should adopt more vigorous measures.[79]

When the new assembly met in March, 1756, General Shirley's call for troops to serve at Niagara and Crown Point was placed before them by the governor. The burgesses at once pronounced it "impracticable and imprudent" to send troops so far at this time, and the council agreed with them.[80] But on account of the recent massacres on their own frontiers they voted £25,000 and included in the act a provision for drafting militia.[81] This provision, however, was practically valueless, for any one who had been drafted might escape service by paying £10, and we are

[76] *Journals*, 319; *Din. Pap.*, ii, 269.

[77] Feb. 23, 1756. *Din. Pap.*, ii, 339.

[78] Dinwiddie to Halifax, Feb. 24, 1756. *Din. Pap.*, ii, 346. See also p. 339.

[79] To Dinwiddie, April 22, 1756. *Writings* (Ford's ed.) i, 249. On April 16, he had written to John Robinson, Speaker of the House of Burgesses, that the people would do nothing to help themselves. " . . . . the timidity of the inhabitants of this country is to be equaled by nothing but their perverseness. Yesterday was the time appointed for all to meet who were inclined to join for this desirable end, and only fifteen came, some of whom refused to go but upon such terms as must have rendered their services burthensome to the country." *Ibid.*, 241.

[80] *Din. Pap.*, ii, 379-380; *Journals*, 345.

[81] Hening, *Statutes*, vii, 9 et seq.

told by Dinwiddie that many availed themselves of this privilege.[82] No drafted troops could be taken to serve outside of the province. As other colonies had similar laws restricting their troops to service within their own borders, offensive warfare was practically impossible. Discipline was equally impossible under existing laws. Deserters turned their guns against their own officers and defied their authority.[83] "They go off in twenties," wrote Washington, "and all threaten to return (home), if they are not relieved in a very short time or discharged."[84] Desertion was made easier by the connivance and assistance of the very inhabitants who most needed protection.[85] The feeling of common interest was so utterly lacking that the inhabitants of one county would refuse aid to those of another.[86]

In the matter of money Virginia was liberal for the time. Even Dinwiddie admitted that the burgesses had granted as much as the colony could afford, and more than the assembly of any other colony;[87] but at best they were "only keeping the expedition alive." Each colony preferred to act by itself and in its own way, therefore little was accomplished.[88] As a result of the militia laws in force the enemy could attack one province at a time without fear of being molested by troops from another colony. The feeling in Virginia is well illustrated by her vote of £8,000 for enlisting troops for the king's regiment of Royal Americans and

[82] *Corresp. of Gov. Sharpe*, i, 444.

[83] Washington, *Writings* (Ford's ed.) i, 269-276.

[84] *Ibid.*, 286. On October 10, 1756, he wrote Dinwiddie: "The militia are under such bad order and discipline, that they will go and come when and where they please, consulting solely their own inclinations." *Writings*, i, 357.

[86] "When Hampshire was invaded," wrote Washington to Lord Fairfax, "and called on Frederick for assistance the people of the latter refused their aid, answering, 'Let them defend themselves, as we shall do if they come to us.' Now the enemy have forced through that county, and begin to infest this, those a little removed from danger are equally infatuated; and will be, I fear, until all in turn fall a sacrifice to an insulting and merciless enemy." *Writings*, i, 331.

[85] *Ibid.*, 326; *Pa. Arch.*, ser. 2, ii, 694.

[87] *Din. Pap.*, ii, 420. Up to June, 1756, Virginia had granted at various times £150,000. *Ibid.*, 437.

[88] *Corresp. of Gov. Sharpe*, i, 407. Sharpe to Albermarle, May 5, 1756.

transporting them to New York, accompanied by a refusal to permit a single man to be drafted for that service.[89] No authority, no emergency could induce the burgesses to yield what they considered their constitutional rights. Men who enjoyed, as they claimed to do, "the Blessings of a *British* Constitution, reduced to its original Purity"[90] could hardly be expected to submit to compulsory military service.

The relations between governor and assembly during the year 1757 seem to have been more harmonious than usual. At the close of the session, which lasted from April to June, the governor informed Sharpe that the assembly had "generously granted every Thing" he had asked of them.[91] They voted to increase their regiment to 1200 men and granted £80,000 to maintain them. An additional sum of £3,000 was voted for the purpose of buying presents for the Indians. In order to complete the regiment, drafting was permitted, but again it was restricted to non-freeholders—that is, "vagrants and dissolute persons." Two companies were to be sent to assist South Carolina, and two additional companies if the British commander should deem it necessary.[92] This was a notable departure from their former exclusive policy, but as these troops were all vagrants their "rights" were not quite so sacred. Pitt's vigorous war policy and a promise of reimbursement seem to have impressed the assembly favorably. But recruiting was still difficult. Washington despaired of filling the ranks unless the officers were permitted to enlist indentured servants.[93]

Another act passed during this session imposed the death penalty for mutiny and desertion,[94] and still another provided for mustering, training and equipping the militia for defense within the province.[95] They still refused to subject their troops

[89] *Din. Pap.*, ii, 524.

[90] *Journals*, 404.

[91] *Din. Pap.*, ii, 639; *Corresp. of Gov. Sharpe*, ii, 25.

[92] Hening, *Statutes*, vii, 70, 75.

[93] *Writings*, i, 474.

[94] Hening, *Statutes*, vii, 87 et seq.

[95] *Ibid.*, 93 et seq.

to regular British army discipline,[96] but the provisions adopted
marked a distinct advance over the old regulations. Another
element of discord was removed during the same year when Dinwiddie ordered Fort Cumberland evacuated. It was thought
that the Maryland assembly would provide for this post, but
they indignantly refused to do so.[97]

In 1758 the burgesses adopted a still more liberal policy.
They voted to augment the forces of the colony to 2000 men to
be used wherever the British commanding officer should think
best.[98] Money was freely voted at both sessions held during that
year. This policy was continued during the remaining years of
the war. There had been a heavy drain on the resources of the
colony and the money grants were not large, but a greater spirit
of liberality was shown in putting the troops under control of
British generals to be used in offensive warfare.

By too jealously guarding the rights of freeholders and the
special interests of their own province, the burgesses had seriously impaired the military efficiency of the colony, but on the
whole their conduct compared favorably with that of the neighboring governments. The valuable services rendered toward
the close of the war only emphasized the necessity of some general
authority with adequate power to act in military affairs, unham-
pered by local prejudices.

NORTH CAROLINA

In North Carolina conditions were not favorable for active
participation in the war. A jealous guarding of charter rights,[99]
factious disputes, and a vicious financial system all tended to
prevent a proper support of the general cause.

---

[96] *Din. Pap.*, ii, 692. Dinwiddie to Gov. Littleton of S. C., Aug. 27, 1757.

[97] Washington, *Writings*, i, 434, notes.

[98] Hening, *Statutes*, vii, 163 et seq.

[99] The charter granted by Charles II was liberal, and after it had been
abrogated in 1728 the assembly still claimed rights under it. "To them,
Magna Charta, 'the great charter,' was not the one granted by King John
to the English Barons at Runnymede, but the one granted by Charles the
Second to the Lords Proprietors of the Province of Carolina." Prefatory
notes to vol. vi, *Col. Rec. of N. C.*, p. iii.

Some energy was displayed by the assembly at the beginning
of the war, North Carolina being the first[100] to send aid to Virginia when that colony was making preparations to repel the
French. Unfortunately this aid proved of little value. In
March, 1754, the assembly voted 750 men for the assistance of
Virginia, and £12,000 for their maintenance,[1] but it was proclamation money which Dinwiddie pronounced "nearly worthless."[2]
The officers were unable to raise the whole number of troops
voted, but those who did enlist were joined to the British independent companies without opposition and paid a larger allowance than troops of other colonies. The assembly doubtless meant
well in allowing large pay to the troops, but as a result of this
and the slowness of recruiting the money was spent before the
troops were ready for service, and they became a burden rather
than an aid to Virginia. The officers of the independent companies would not serve under Virginia officers and the troops
deserted as soon as the money was gone.[3]

Recruiting in North Carolina as in other colonies was slow
and difficult. Little power was given to the governor to enforce
the few regulations which had been established by law. A law
was passed authorizing the drafting of unmarried men, but they
avoided the draft by open defiance or hiding. County officials
neglected or refused to make proper returns to the governor,
thereby aiding the delinquents and nullifying the laws in a great
measure.[4] It should be noted, however, that when the assembly
did vote troops they did not restrict the place and time of
their service.[5] North Carolina stood quite alone in this freedom
from local prejudice.

100 *Din. Pap.*, i, 162.

1 *Col. Rec. of N. C.*, v, 738. Jas. Abercromby to Board of Trade.

2 So much complaint was made by British merchants because this money
was made a legal tender in the province that in 1759 the Privy Council
ordered Governor Dobbs to recommend the repeal of the legal tender law.
Col. Rec. of N. C., vi, 43-45.

3 Dinwiddie to Secretary Fox, July 24, 1754; Same to Secretary Robinson, Sept. 23. *Din. Pap.*, i, 246, 327.

4 *Col. Rec. of N. C.*, v, 571. Dobbs to Board of Trade, March 15, 1756.

5 *Ibid.*, 738-739. Abercromby to Board of Trade.

Factional quarrels continued through nearly the entire period of the war. At first the trouble was not with the governor, but hostile factions were contending for supremacy. Governor Dobbs wrote that when he came to the colony he "found it had been divided into Parties, and in a very low state; and one-half of the Province not obeying the laws made by the other, nor attending the Assemblies, refusing to pay the Taxes which the Assembly raised, so that the Colony was in debt, and obliged upon the present breaking out of this war to raise £40,000 in paper of this Currency (£30,000 Sterling) which half of this Province would not receive nor circulate."[6]

But disputes between governor and assembly were not wanting. In January, 1759, Governor Dobbs complained to the Board of Trade that the lower house claimed full control over all money voted by themselves as well as that granted by Parliament.[7] The lower house in May of that year voted £6,000 for troops, but the money was to be controlled by themselves. The bill was rejected by the governor and council after futile attempts to induce the lower house to alter it.[8] The lower house then preferred a series of charges against the governor. Among other things he was accused of illegally collecting license fees, and of taking a toll from the money sent from England. He had without lawful authority appointed his nephew paymaster with no duty except to collect these fees. The money already voted had, they said, been wasted by incompetent officers appointed by the governor.[9] No doubt there was much truth in these charges; at any rate they served as an excuse for exclusive control of finances by the lower house. Both sides were censured by the Lords of Trade for haggling over trivial points at such a time, and Dobbs was especially criticised for attempting to dictate the choice of an agent to represent the colony in England.[10] Similar disputes

---

[6] *Col. Rec. of N. C.*, v, 595. Dobbs to Loudoun, July 10, 1756.

[7] *Ibid.*, vi, 1-7.

[8] *Ibid.*, 32.

[9] *Ibid.*, 410 et seq.

[10] *Ibid.*, 538 et seq. Board of Trade to Dobbs, April 4, 1761.

occupied the time during the first session of 1760, and after
several failures to agree, a bill was finally passed in June for
raising 300 men.[11] That so small an amount of money was sent
them from England the assembly attributed to the want of an
agent in London;[12] and they had no agent at this time because
Dobbs claimed the right to dictate the choice. In the spring of
1761 the lower house attached the appointment of an agent as a
rider to a bill granting £20,000 for the king's service. But the
house lacked the resisting power possessed by some of its con-
temporaries, and when this bill was rejected by the governor and
council they withdrew the rider and granted the money.[13] As the
war soon ended nothing further was asked of them. Discord continued, but the disputes were now confined to local matters.

SOUTH CAROLINA

Before the war period the South Carolina governor had been
deprived of many of the powers usually enjoyed by the governor
in other colonies. The war, therefore, did not materially alter
the situation. The council had already curtailed his legislative
powers and the lower house had usurped the power of appointing
administrative officials.[14] James Glen, who had assumed the
government in 1743, attempted to regain the lost powers but with
little success. The claim of the commons (lower house) that their
money bills must be passed or rejected by the council caused
discord between the two houses. A dispute on this question
arose in 1756 over the refusal of the council to concur in a bill
granting £41,000 for a frontier fort and other purposes. Glen
seems to have resented the usurpations of the council more than
those of the commons, for in this matter he gave his support to
the latter. A writer of the time—champion of the commons—
proved to his own satisfaction, and doubtless to that of the

---

11 *Col. Rec. of N. C.*, vi, 257, 266.

12 *Ibid.*, 477.

13 *Ibid.*, 654, 659.

14 McCrady, *South Carolina under the Royal Government*, 254-259.

people, that the council had no legitimate claim to the functions of an upper legislative house.[15]

Like other southern colonies South Carolina did not take a very active part in defending the British domains. The British independent company of 300 men which she supported participated with the Virginia forces in the battle of Great Meadows, and £6,000 was voted for the Braddock expedition,[16] but during the greater part of the war her activities were confined principally to the defense of her own frontiers. Disputes between the assembly and Governor Glen delayed action even on the frontiers, and little had been accomplished when he retired from power in June of 1756.[17]

The currency of the colony was so badly depreciated[18] that the money voted was practically worthless as a purchasing medium. As there was practically no metal money in the province and Governor Glen would not sign bills for increasing the amount of currency, little effective aid could be given while he remained in office. Even Dinwiddie criticised Glen for adhering too closely to his instructions[19] and thereby obstructing money grants; but private grievances no doubt influenced the former's opinion as the two men were not on the best of terms.

Greater harmony prevailed during the administration of Governor Littleton. Money was voted for frontier forts and British army rules of discipline were adopted for the troops of the colony.[20] The latter measure was remarkable for the time as other colonies jealously guarded the privilege of maintaining discipline in their own way.

GEORGIA

Little military assistance could be expected from Georgia,

---

[15] McCrady, *op. cit.*, 282-287.

[16] *Din. Pap.*, i, 249. Dinwiddie to Earl of Granville.

[17] *Din. Pap.*, ii, 508.

[18] Dinwiddie stated in a letter to Hamilton, April 27, 1754, that £100,000 S. C. money was not quite equal to £20,000 in Va. currency. *Din. Pap.*, i, 143.

[19] *Din. Pap.*, ii, 28, 29.

[20] *Ibid.*, 508, 692.

for she was unable to protect even her own borders. When in 1755 Governor Reynolds placed before the commons house a letter from Secretary Robinson asking for aid, that body replied that if their "Abilitys were equal to their (our) Inclination" they would contribute liberally, but they were able to "contribute Little or Nothing either as to men or Money" to the general defense.[21] On the contrary they requested the governor to ask the king for means of defense.[22]

Their military weakness was not exaggerated, for as late as 1757 their entire army consisted of forty rangers of their own and a few troops sent there from the independent companies of South Carolina. Their forts were in such a dilapidated condition that on celebration days the guns had to be taken from them for fear the shock of the discharge would cause them to collapse.[23]

While Georgia figured little in disputes over war supplies, she furnished another phase of the controversy over constitutional rights which was both interesting and unique.

Georgia became a royal colony in 1755 and therefore did not possess a long list of accumulated "rights" which must be respected. The task of her legislature was to procure rights and privileges, not to preserve old ones.

Profiting by the example of other rebellious colonies the British government circumscribed the privileges of the Georgia assembly within very narrow limits. The usual privilege of admitting members at their discretion and fixing the qualifications for voters was denied the commons—lower house of assembly —and large powers were given to the governor. Naturally this was resented by the commons. They first asked for privileges usual in American governments, and when the request was denied they proceeded to assume them in defiance of authority.

During the very first session of the assembly under the new government they prepared a series of remonstrances to be sent to the king. They complained that the fixing of fees of public

---

[21] *Col. Rec. of Ga.,* xiii, 47.

[22] *Ibid.,* 61.

[23] *Ibid.,* 130. Report of a committee, Jan. 25, 1757.

offices is entirely in the hands of the governor and council, and asked that such fees be ''settled by Act of General Assembly and not otherwise as is the Custom of all your Majesty's other Provinces in America.''[24]   The royal instructions required that all voters must possess a freehold of at least 50 acres of land, and no one could be a member of the commons house unless he possessed a freehold of 500 acres.   Both of these requirements were opposed by the commons.   They asked for the privilege of fixing qualifications in both cases by law.[25]   At first the governor approved these requests and expressed a desire to have them granted,[26] but when he received a negative reply from England he immediately adopted the English point of view.

The governor's instructions also required him to see that the number of members in the commons should neither be increased nor diminished, but before the commons received an answer to their remonstrance they proceeded to unseat members at will and thereby cut down the membership.[27]   As soon as the governor heard from England he announced the new policy of the ministry.   The ministry admitted that by ''long Usage'' other colonies were exercising the privileges desired by the commons of Georgia, but they also declared such practices to be ''inconsistent with all Colony Constitution whatever, contrary . . . . to the Express direction of His Majesty's Commission, by which alone this Assembly is Constituted.''[28]   Here is a direct denial of all inherent rights, and an announcement that colonial rights in future must be limited to concessions made by royal instructions.   In Georgia this new policy could be first and most easily applied, for a new form of government was just being instituted.

The governor informed the commons that none of their acts would be considered valid until they had complied with the king's instructions, but his warnings were unheeded.   When

---

[24] *Col. Rec. of Ga.*, xiii, 72-73.

[25] *Ibid.*, 73-75.

[26] *Ibid.*

[27] *Ibid.*, 91-92.   Message to assembly, Feb. 12, 1756.

[28] *Ibid.*, 92.

the governor adjourned the assembly for refusing to comply with his demands, the commons held the speaker in the chair by force, and, proceeding to transact business regardless of the governor's order, compelled the speaker to affix his signature. The books of the clerk were seized and the records altered to suit the commons.[29] For a time all communications between the two branches of government ceased, and the governor ended the controversy by dissolving the commons and calling a new election. The commons did not again resort to such violent measures. At various times they claimed privileges which the governor under his instructions was unable to allow, but as no contributions were asked of them comparative harmony prevailed during the remainder of the war period.

That the colonial administrative system of England—if indeed it can be said that there was any system—was inadequate and impotent was apparent to every one whose duty it was to carry it into operation. The acts of defiance, evasion, and insubordination in the colonies during the war had made this sufficiently clear. In nearly every clash of authority the colonists had been victorious, that is, they had either secured that for which they contended or subverted the plans of the prerogative party. Each colony had its own peculiar interests and was indifferent in a great measure to questions of general welfare. The colonists were glad that they were Englishmen and there is no evidence of a conscious desire for independence. They were even willing to contribute aid to the common defense, provided it could be done in their own way. It must, however, be accepted as a free gift with a distinct understanding that coercion was unlawful and not to be tolerated. Royal or proprietary instructions which abridged this freedom were resented and ignored. A refusal to obey instructions naturally led to denial of authority to issue them. The degree of freedom from authority demanded by some of the colonies was incompatible with the status of dependencies as generally understood at the time. The

---

[29] *Col. Rec. of Ga.*, xiii, 99-101. Message of the governor, Feb. 19, 1756, and statement of the speaker.

degree of liberty demanded could be secured only by virtual independence. England recognized this fact more clearly than the colonies did and was preparing to check these independent tendencies.

It is easy to look back and see that instead of employing coercive measures England might have been more successful had she adopted an autonomous colonial system like that in force in Canada and other colonies today. Nothing of the kind could have reasonably been expected in the middle of the eighteenth century. Such a relation between colonies and mother country was yet unknown, and England naturally adopted the policy with which she was most familiar.

Colonial governors, British generals, and British administrative officers had but one remedy to offer, and from the beginning of the war this was urged upon the home government on every possible occasion. Their remedy was parliamentary control and parliamentary taxation to support it. This, they urged, was the only method of insuring obedience and order in the colonies. The attempt of Parliament to act upon this advice and inaugurate a new system, it is needless to add, led directly to the Revolution.

Briefly surveying the struggle already given in detail, it may be observed that the extent of opposition to imperial government varied considerably in different colonies, and increased in proportion to the amount of outside restraint. In Connecticut and Rhode Island where the people enjoyed virtual independence they were usually public spirited and ready to coöperate with the mother country. Proprietary colonies on the other hand, subject to double restrictions from proprietor and king, were the ones which did most to obstruct imperial administration. In later years this might have pointed the way to a successful solution of the administrative problems, but it could hardly be expected that Great Britain at that time would adopt the homeopathic treatment of permitting greater freedom in order to forestall independence.

No summarized statement of the degree of autonomy and the

grounds upon which it was based can be made that will apply to all of the colonies separately. Both depended in a great measure on local conditions and the relation of each individual colony to the mother country. By combining items, however, it is possible to state what the colonies collectively demanded from the central administrative authority. The colonies as a rule kept in close touch with controversies in other places, therefore independent views of any particular assembly soon found an echo in the neighboring provinces.

Except in colonies where the people elected all officers the popular branch of the legislature claimed exclusive control over financial matters. All money voted was a free gift of the people, therefore money bills must not be amended. If all money granted was a free gift, it followed that the peoples' representatives should have the exclusive right to determine how it should be raised—that is, the right to dictate the method and extent of taxation. They also claimed exclusive control of the raising, disciplining, and the movement of colonial troops. Many colonies as we have seen, were inclined to restrict their troops to defensive service within their own borders, making defensive warfare difficult and offensive campaigns practically impossible. The privilege of adjourning at will, wholesome in itself, was often abused by assemblies in critical times.

They based their claim to exclusive control of financial matters on precedent and the "rights of Englishmen." Parliament possessed this right in England and, being Englishmen, the colonists claimed a similar right for their assemblies, within their own jurisdiction. As Parliament did not represent Englishmen in America its taxing power did not extend to America. In short, they desired all the rights of Englishmen, but comparatively few of the duties. Some colonies claimed additional rights based on their charters, and held that such rights once given were an irrevocable bar against both king and Parliament. In this they made no distinction between rights and privileges. All maintained that their "rights as Englishmen" and "natural right" entitled them to the privileges of government without any outside interference with their internal affairs. In a word, they had developed practically all the arguments that were used after the passage of the Stamp Act.

Whether and to what extent the claims of the colonists were just we need not here discuss. The significant fact is that they were radically incompatible with the British colonial policy, one of which must give way. The American ideal was government by the consent of the governed. Like all Anglo-Saxons they did not take kindly to the role of a subject people. Prerogative they were unwilling to recognize. England had either to recognize this ideal and be satisfied with nominal sovereignty or the ideal must be shattered by a reorganization of the colonial system. Aside from the new general policy of George III and his Tory supporters and the changed conditions caused by the expulsion of the French, the defiance of the colonies and the inability of England to enforce its authority were sufficient to make alterations in the old system desirable if not imperative.

The attempt at reorganization lies without the scope of this paper. It began as soon as the war ended and resulted in the independence of the colonies. The colonies were prepared to meet the issue. During the seven years of controversy they had formulated their theories and were now ready to defend them. There was a unity of ideas, but up to this time there had been no unity of strength and action. Added pressure by the antagonist was certain to produce such a unity. So long as the policy of England remained weak and vacillating; so long as the administration was left to individual governors whose means of subsistence depended on the good will of the colonies themselves, each assembly was able to cope with the situation and preferred to do so. Up to this time local prejudice outweighed any desire for union. But when Parliament assumed control and began to subject the colonies to one general scheme of taxation and administration, concerted action on the part of the colonies became necessary. This characteristic marks the principal change of conditions after the passage of the Stamp Act. Unity of action was practically the only new element. Their doctrines, theories, and arguments were the same; the policy of England, not that of the colonies, had changed. A more definite policy of England simply caused a united resistance, and at last the colonies came to see that nothing but independence could procure for them the desired freedom from restraint.

LIST OF AUTHORITIES.

ARNOLD, S. G.
History of the State of Rhode Island. New York, 1860. 2 vols.

BANCROFT, GEORGE.
History of the United States; ed. 22. Boston 1872. 10 vols.

BANCROFT, GEORGE.
History of the United States; last revision. New York, 1882. 6 vols.

BEER, G. L.
British Colonial Policy, 1754-1765. New York, 1907.

BURNABY, ANDREW.
Travels in North America, in Pinkerton, Voyages and Travels. London,
1812. Vol. 13.

Collections of the Massachusetts Historical Society; ser. 1. Boston, 1795,
1801. Vols. 4, 7.

Colonial Records of Connecticut. Hartford, 1877, 1880. Vols. 10, 11.

Colonial Records of the State of Georgia. Atlanta, 1907. Vol. 13.

Colonial Records of North Carolina. Raleigh, 1887, 1888. Vols. 5, 6.

Dinwiddie Papers, 1751-1758. Richmond, 1883, 1894. 2 vols. In Collections of the Virginia Historical Society; new ser., vols. 3, 4.

FISHER, DANIEL.
Extracts from the Diary of; in Pennsylvania Magazine of History.
Philadelphia, 1893. Vol. 17.

FISHER, S. G.
Pennsylvania Colony and Commonwealth. Philadelphia, 1897.

FRANKLIN BENJAMIN.
Works; Sparks ed. Boston, 1840.

HENING, WILLIAM W.
Statutes at Large of Virginia. Richmond, 1819, 1820. Vols. 6, 7.

HUTCHINSON, THOMAS.
The History of the Province of Massachusetts Bay. London, 1828. 3 vols.

Journals of the House of Burgesses of Virginia, 1752-1758. Richmond, 1909.

McCRADY, EDWARD.
The History of South Carolina under the Royal Government, 1719-1776.
New York, 1899.

McLAUGHLIN, A. C.
The Confederation and Constitution, in Hart, A.B., The American Nation.
New York, 1905. Vol. 10.

New Hampshire Provincial Papers. Manchester, 1872. Vol. 6.

New Jersey Archives; ser. 1. Newark, 1885. Vols. 8, 9.

New York Colonial History Documents. Albany, 1855, 1856. Vols. 6, 7.

Pennsylvania Archives, 1748-1756, 1756-1760. Philadelphia, 1853.

Pennsylvania Archives; ser. 2. Harrisburg, 1877. Vol. 6.

Pennsylvania Colonial Records. Harrisburg, 1851, 1852. Vols. 5, 6, 7, 8, 9.

Review of Military Operations in North-America, from 1753 to 1756; in *Collections of the Massachusetts Historical Society,* ser. 1. Boston, 1801. Vol. 7.

SHARPE, Governor HORATIO.
   Correspondence. 3 vols. Baltimore, 1888, 1890. In *Maryland Archives.*

WASHINGTON GEORGE.
   Writings; Ford ed. New York, 1889.